KYOTO TRAVEL

2024

Complete Colored Guide To Explore Hidden Treasures, Cuisine, History, Culture, Top Destinations and Best Day Travels Full of Insider Tips and Tricks To Save Money.

Richard Caraway

Disclaimer:

The information provided in this travel guide, "Tokyo Travel Guide 2024," is for general informational purposes only. While every effort has been made to present accurate and up-to-date information, the author and publisher make no warranties regarding the completeness, reliability, or suitability of the information contained herein. Readers are advised to use this guide as a reference and exercise their own judgment in making travel decisions. The author and publisher shall not be held responsible for any inconvenience, loss, injury, or damage incurred as a result of using the information presented in this guide. Travelers are encouraged to verify crucial details such as schedules, prices, and availability directly with relevant establishments or authorities before planning their trip.

Contents

INTRODUCTION...6

CHAPTER 1..9

WELCOME TO KYOTO...9

   OVERVIEW OF KYOTO..9

   KYOTO'S CLIMATE AND WEATHER.........................10

   BEST TIME TO VISIT KYOTO...................................13

   HOW TO GET TO KYOTO..15

CHAPTER 2..18

HISTORY OF KYOTO..18

   EARLY HISTORY OF KYOTO...................................18

   KYOTO DURING THE EDO PERIOD.......................22

   KYOTO DURING THE MEIJI PERIOD......................24

CHAPTER 3..27

KYOTO'S CULTURAL HERITAGE................................27

   OVERVIEW OF KYOTO'S CULTURAL HERITAGE...27

   TRADITIONAL ARTS AND CRAFTS OF KYOTO......30

   KYOTO'S GEISHA CULTURE.................................32

   KYOTO'S TRADITIONAL FESTIVALS......................35

CHAPTER 4..38

TOP DESTINATIONS IN KYOTO AND WHAT TO DO....38

   KINKAKU-JI (GOLDEN PAVILION)...........................38

   FUSHIMI INARI TAISHA..42

   ARASHIYAMA BAMBOO GROVE............................44

   KIYOMIZU-DERA...45

   GION DISTRICT..47

   NIJO CASTLE...49

   KYOTO IMPERIAL PALACE.....................................51

   NISHIKI MARKET..53

   TOEI KYOTO STUDIO PARK...................................55

CHAPTER 5... 58

KYOTO'S TEMPLES AND SHRINES.............................58

   OVERVIEW OF KYOTO'S TEMPLES AND SHRINES..
58

   MUST-SEE TEMPLES IN KYOTO..............................60

   MUST-SEE SHRINES IN KYOTO............................. 65

   HIDDEN GEMS: LESSER-KNOWN TEMPLES AND
SHRINES...68

CHAPTER 6.. 71

KYOTO'S GARDENS AND PARKS................................71

   OVERVIEW OF KYOTO'S GARDENS AND PARKS..71

   MUST-SEE GARDENS IN KYOTO............................73

   MUST-SEE PARKS IN KYOTO................................. 77

   HIDDEN GEMS: LESSER-KNOWN GARDENS AND
PARKS.. 80

CHAPTER 7.. 84

KYOTO'S MUSEUMS AND GALLERIES.......................84

   OVERVIEW OF KYOTO'S MUSEUMS AND
GALLERIES... 84

   MUST-SEE MUSEUMS IN KYOTO...........................85

   MUST-SEE GALLERIES IN KYOTO......................... 87

   HIDDEN GEMS: LESSER-KNOWN MUSEUMS AND
GALLERIES... 89

CHAPTER 8.. 92

KYOTO'S FOOD AND DRINK.. 92

   OVERVIEW OF KYOTO'S FOOD AND DRINK SCENE
92

   Overview of Kyoto's Food and Drink Scene:.............. 92

   MUST-TRY DISHES IN KYOTO................................94

   BEST RESTAURANTS IN KYOTO............................98

   BEST BARS AND CAFES IN KYOTO..................... 102

CHAPTER 9.. 107

KYOTO'S SHOPPING SCENE..................................... 107

OVERVIEW OF KYOTO'S SHOPPING SCENE...... 107

BEST SHOPPING DISTRICTS IN KYOTO............. 109

MUST-VISIT MARKETS IN KYOTO........................ 114

BEST SOUVENIRS TO BUY IN KYOTO................. 118

CHAPTER 10... **122**

KYOTO'S FESTIVALS AND EVENTS........................... **122**

MUST-SEE FESTIVALS IN KYOTO........................ 122

MUST-SEE EVENTS IN KYOTO............................ 125

HIDDEN GEMS: LESSER-KNOWN FESTIVALS AND
EVENTS..128

CHAPTER 11...**131**

KYOTO'S SURROUNDING AREAS............................. **131**

DAY TRIPS FROM KYOTO.................................... 131

BEST PLACES TO STAY OUTSIDE KYOTO........... 142

HIDDEN GEMS: LESSER-KNOWN DESTINATIONS
NEAR KYOTO... 147

CHAPTER 12... **151**

IMPORTANT INFORMATION.....................................**151**

MONEY SAVING TIPS WHILE AT KYOTO.............. 151

SUMMARY OF KYOTO AT A GLANCE....................153

GETTING AROUND KYOTO....................................154

HOW TO STAY SAFE IN KYOTO............................155

WHEN TO VISIT KYOTO... 157

KYOTO TRAVEL RESTRICTIONS............................ 158

JAPAN VISA.. 158

WHERE TO EXCHANGE CURRENCY.................... 159

KYOTO PACKING LIST..160

INTRODUCTION

Kyoto holds a magnetic charm unlike any other in Japan. Nestled amidst breathtaking mountain vistas, this city is a treasure trove of Zen gardens, temples steeped in Buddhist and Shinto traditions, winding hiking trails, and even some of the finest sake distilleries you'll find. And let's not forget the delectable cuisine that's a feast for the taste buds! My time in Kyoto was an enchanting blend of exploration, from wandering through temples to marveling at an array of gardens and strolling through the serene bamboo forest.

Believe me, Kyoto lives up to every bit of praise you've heard. It's a destination on everyone's must-visit list, drawing both international travelers and locals alike. Yes, you'll encounter crowds, especially during peak seasons, but trust me, braving the masses is absolutely worth it. And fear not, I've got plenty of insider tips to help you navigate and avoid the hustle and bustle, ensuring you savor every moment.

Three days in Kyoto? That's my recommendation. But let me tell you, Kyoto isn't just another stop on the itinerary for me. It's my absolute favorite city in Japan, a sentiment that's held steadfast over the years. Tokyo and Osaka might offer more frenetic excitement, but Kyoto? It's where Japan's essence truly resides. The city's pace, unhurried and deliberate, transports you to an era that feels steeped in history.

Kyoto isn't just a city; it's a living canvas adorned with Buddhist temples, Shinto shrines, the grace of geishas, and meticulously crafted gardens, a world away from the sensory overload of Harajuku or Akihabara. Sure, I appreciate video games and the Otaku culture, but when I think of everything I adore about Japan—its ambiance, traditions, culture, and above all, its food—Kyoto is the vivid picture that fills my mind.

This travel guide? It's your key to unlocking the very best of Kyoto, ensuring you experience its finest offerings while also making savvy savings along the way. It's brimming with my personal insights, tricks, and recommendations, crafted to ensure every moment in Kyoto is nothing short of extraordinary. Embrace it, relish it, and above all, have a safe and splendid journey. I'm rooting for you!

CHAPTER 1

WELCOME TO KYOTO

OVERVIEW OF KYOTO

Kyoto is a city located in the central part of Japan's main island, Honshu. It is the capital city of Kyoto Prefecture and has a population of over 1.4 million people. Kyoto is known for its rich cultural heritage, beautiful temples and shrines, and stunning natural scenery. It is a popular destination for both domestic and international tourists.

Kyoto was the capital of Japan for over 1,000 years, from 794 to 1868, and is considered the birthplace of Japanese culture.

The city is home to over 2,000 temples and shrines, many of which are UNESCO World Heritage sites . Some of the most popular attractions in Kyoto include Kinkaku-ji (the Golden Pavilion), Fushimi Inari Shrine, and Kiyomizu-dera Temple. Kyoto is also known for its traditional arts and crafts, such as pottery, calligraphy, and tea ceremony. Visitors can take classes or workshops to learn more about these fascinating traditions.

In addition to its cultural attractions, Kyoto is also a great destination for foodies. The city is famous for its kaiseki cuisine, which is a multi-course meal that features seasonal ingredients and beautiful presentation. Kyoto is also known for its matcha (green tea) and wagashi (traditional Japanese sweets).

Overall, Kyoto is a wonderful destination for travelers who are interested in Japanese culture, history, and natural beauty.

KYOTO'S CLIMATE AND WEATHER

Kyoto has a temperate humid climate with quite mild winters and hot, moist, and rainy summers. The city is affected by the monsoon circulation: in winter, the northwest cold currents will prevail, while in summer, they will be replaced by hot and humid currents of tropical origin. The city is located about 50 kilometers (30 miles) away from the sea, in a plain surrounded by low mountains, and to the south, it is practically merged with Osaka and Kobe, in a large metropolitan area called Keihanshin.

Winter is the driest season, at least in quantity; the rainiest months are June and July, i.e., the first period of the rainy season (called Baiu). August is the hottest month, both because of the thermal inertia of the sea and because of the lower frequency of periods of bad weather . The amount of sunshine in Kyoto, all things considered, is decent in winter, but it never becomes very good, however, there are two relative maxima, one in spring (April-May) and the other in August, after the Baiu rains, both with around 6 hours of sunshine per day.

BEST TIME TO VISIT KYOTO

Kyoto experiences a temperate humid climate, characterized by mild winters and hot, moist, and rainy summers. The ideal times to visit Kyoto are during spring (March to May) and autumn (September to November). These seasons offer mild and comfortable weather without the need for superscripts. Spring showcases beautiful cherry blossoms, while autumn boasts vibrant foliage.

However, these peak seasons tend to be the busiest, resulting in higher hotel rates and limited availability. To avoid crowds, consider visiting Kyoto during winter (mid-December to February) when the city is quieter and blanketed in snow. Winter visitors benefit from more lodging options and discounted rates due to the off-season.

Summer (June to August) marks the rainy season in Kyoto, characterized by hot and humid weather. Despite this, summer also heralds numerous festivals throughout the city, creating an unforgettable calendar of celebrations. If you can tolerate the heat and humidity, exploring Kyoto's diverse neighborhoods during summer offers a chance to immerse yourself in its vibrant culture.

HOW TO GET TO KYOTO

Nestled in the heart of Japan's Kansai region, reaching Kyoto is a journey into Japan's rich cultural tapestry. Whether arriving from bustling Tokyo or internationally, several transportation options seamlessly connect travelers to this historical gem.

By Air:

Kyoto doesn't have its own airport, but the nearest major gateway is Osaka's Kansai International Airport (KIX), located approximately 75 minutes away by express train. Alternatively, Osaka's Itami Airport (ITM) serves domestic flights and is about an hour away from Kyoto by bus or train.

From Tokyo:

Travelers coming from Tokyo can opt for the Shinkansen (bullet train), an iconic experience in itself. The JR Tokaido Shinkansen connects Tokyo Station to Kyoto Station in about 2 hours and 20 minutes, whisking passengers across the scenic landscapes of Japan at speeds of up to 300 km/h (186 mph).

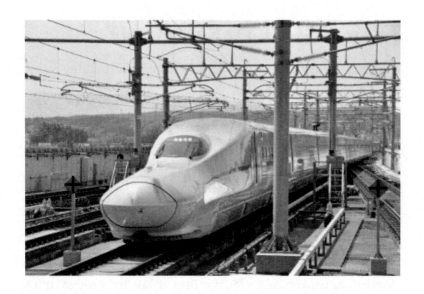

By Train:

Kyoto Station is a major transportation hub that connects various parts of Japan with regular train services. JR West operates express and local trains, making it easy to get to from nearby cities such as Osaka, Kobe, and Nara.

By Bus:

Long-distance buses are a cost-effective option, with overnight services from major cities such as Tokyo and Hiroshima. These buses provide a comfortable and cost-effective mode of transportation, with a variety of amenities onboard.

From Kansai International Airport:

Direct access to Kyoto from Kansai International Airport is available via the Haruka Express, offering a smooth ride to

Kyoto Station. Additionally, limousine buses provide a convenient alternative for travelers with heavier luggage.

Local Transportation:

When you arrive in Kyoto, you can easily navigate the city thanks to an efficient public transportation system that includes buses and subways. Visitors can use prepaid IC cards or one-day passes for unlimited rides to explore Kyoto's cultural hotspots.

The journey to Kyoto is seamless, providing a glimpse into Japan's storied past and vibrant present. With a variety of modes of transportation connecting visitors to this historic city, the journey itself becomes an integral part of the experience, promising an unforgettable introduction to Kyoto's timeless allure.

CHAPTER 2.

HISTORY OF KYOTO

EARLY HISTORY OF KYOTO

Kyoto, Japan's ancient capital, traces its origins back to the 8th century when it was established as Heian-kyo, the capital of Japan in 794 AD. Emperor Kammu chose this location for its strategic significance, nestled in a basin surrounded by protective mountains and bordered by the Kamo and Katsura rivers.

Foundation and Capitalization:
Heian-kyo, meaning "Capital of Peace and Tranquility," was meticulously planned with a grid-like layout, reflecting Chinese urban design principles. This architectural blueprint aimed to symbolize harmony and order within the city, mirroring the ideals of the ruling aristocracy.

Cultural Renaissance:

Under aristocratic rule, the city prospered during the Heian Period (794–1185). Through its integration with politics, culture, and arts it fostered the growth of traditional Japanese literature, poetry (notably the emergence of waka poetry), and courtly traditions. Lady Murasaki Shikibu's

"Tale of Genji" is an iconic representation of Japanese literature, which was crafted in these cultural corridors.

Shrines and Temples:

In this period, the city's topography underwent a transformation as well as the construction of iconic temples and shrines, including the original buildings of the Fushimi Inari Taisha and Byodoin Temple, which reflect the spirit of spirituality and architecture.

Imperial Legacy:

For more than a millennium, the imperial court was based in Kyoto until it was moved to Tokyo during the Meiji Restoration in 1869. The preservation of Kyoto's historical significance as the center of Japanese civilization is evident in its enduring traditions, historic sites, and respect for its imperial heritage.

Legacy of Early Kyoto:

From its earliest days, Kyoto served as the foundation for Japan's cultural identity and left an indelible mark on its artistic, architectural, and social heritage. The city's role as Japan's cultural and political center has left a lasting impression on the nation, drawing visitors from all over the world to explore its rich history.

The early period of Kyoto was marked by cultural expansion and the establishment of traditions that continue to this day, paving the way for centuries-long displays of culture and history.

KYOTO DURING THE HEIAN PERIOD

During the Heian Period (794-1185), Kyoto, then known as Heian-kyo, emerged as the cultural and political epicenter of Japan. This era, spanning over three centuries, witnessed a profound influence on the city's development, marking a significant cultural renaissance.

Kyoto flourished as a symbol of refined elegance and artistic sophistication during the reign of the imperial court. The courtly rituals, literature, and the pursuit of aesthetic beauty were all fostered by the aristocracy. The meticulously planned layout of the city, inspired by Chinese urban design, represented harmony and order, reflecting the ideals held by the ruling elite.

With the creation of notable literary works, literature became the heartbeat of Heian-kyo. "The Tale of Genji," an epic narrative reflecting courtly life, love, and human emotions written by Lady Murasaki Shikibu, is considered one of the world's first novels. This masterpiece exemplified the complexities of courtly relationships and the nuances of human emotions, influencing Japanese literature for centuries to come.

During this time, art and aesthetics flourished, defining the quintessential Heian culture. Delicate and refined art forms showcased the city's aesthetic sensibilities, such as the colorful and intricate designs of Heian-era clothing and the elegant art of calligraphy. Heian-kyo became a haven for artists, poets, and artisans, encouraging creativity and innovation in a wide range of artistic pursuits.

Religious and spiritual practices were also expressed through the construction of grand temples and shrines, which represented the populace's spiritual devotion. Temples such as the renowned Byodoin Temple and the original structures of Fushimi Inari Taisha served as centers of worship and contemplation in the city's religious landscape.

In Kyoto's history, the Heian Period encapsulated an era of cultural efflorescence and refined elegance. Its lasting legacy can be found in the city's preserved traditions, arts, and architectural wonders. The influence of Heian-kyo on Japanese cultural identity endures, reflecting a golden age of creativity and artistic refinement that continues to captivate visitors exploring Kyoto's rich historical tapestry.

KYOTO DURING THE EDO PERIOD

The Edo Period (1603-1868) ushered in a transformative chapter in Kyoto's history, characterized by a shift in power, cultural evolution, and periods of both prosperity and upheaval.

While Kyoto lost its status as the political capital during this period, it retained its cultural significance as Japan's cultural heart. The Tokugawa shogunate centralized power in Edo (modern-day Tokyo), resulting in a decline in Kyoto's political influence. Nonetheless, the city remained a symbol of tradition, art, and spirituality, serving as the imperial court's residence and preserving its historical heritage.

Kyoto thrived as a center of arts and craftsmanship despite political changes. Traditional industries such as tea ceremony utensil production, weaving, and pottery flourished. Kyoto's artisans and craftsmen honed their skills, creating exquisite ceramics, textiles, and artistic works that became sought-after commodities throughout Japan.

The Edo Period Kyoto witnessed a revival of interest in traditional arts and culture. The streets of the city were alive with activity, with thriving entertainment districts and theaters. Kabuki, a type of traditional Japanese theater, rose to prominence, showcasing dramatic performances that captivated audiences with their elaborate costumes and gripping storytelling.

During this period, the cityscape of Kyoto evolved with the construction of merchant houses, temples, and shrines that reflected changing tastes and architectural styles of the time. While the shogunate's policies restricted new construction in Kyoto, they also resulted in the preservation of many historical sites and districts, which contributed to the city's current UNESCO World Heritage status.

Kyoto experienced both social and economic prosperity as well as challenges. Merchants thrived in the city, fostering a vibrant commercial culture. However, tensions and minor conflicts arose, particularly during times of economic stress or political unrest.

Kyoto experienced a nuanced era during the Edo Period, blending cultural refinement with shifting political dynamics. Despite its political decline, Kyoto remained a pillar of tradition, artistry, and cultural heritage, cultivating an enduring legacy that shapes Kyoto's identity as a cultural treasure trove to this day.

KYOTO DURING THE MEIJI PERIOD

The Meiji Period (1868-1912) in Kyoto's history was a time of profound change, marking Japan's modernization and transition from a feudal society to a rapidly industrializing nation. This period brought seismic shifts, altering the city's landscape, culture, and societal norms.

The Meiji Restoration marked the end of the Tokugawa shogunate and the return of imperial rule. Kyoto, as the imperial capital during this transitional period, once again played a pivotal role, hosting significant political and social reforms.

The relocation of the imperial capital from Kyoto to Tokyo was one of the most notable changes, signaling a symbolic shift in Japan's political center. While this reduced Kyoto's political standing, it relieved the city of administrative duties, allowing it to refocus on preserving its rich cultural heritage.

Kyoto's economy and industries were transformed as a result of modernization efforts. The city embraced technological progress and industrialization, which resulted in the establishment of modern factories and industries alongside traditional crafts. As the city adapted to changing times while preserving its cultural legacy, this juxtaposition created a unique blend of the old and the new.

Western influence began to permeate Kyoto, bringing new ideas, educational systems, and cultural exchanges with it. Western architecture, education, and fashion were introduced to the city, influencing artistic and societal norms.

Kyoto's historical landmarks and cultural assets were also preserved and restored during the Meiji Period. Efforts were made to safeguard and promote the city's temples, shrines, and traditional arts, recognizing their importance in shaping Japan's identity.

Despite the winds of change, Kyoto's dedication to preserving its cultural heritage has remained unwavering. The city emerged as a keeper of tradition in a rapidly modernizing nation, retaining its status as Japan's cultural soul.

Kyoto's Meiji Period represents a complex interplay between tradition and modernity, as the city navigated the challenges and opportunities of a changing society. This period established Kyoto's identity as a city where the past and present coexist harmoniously, inviting visitors to explore its rich tapestry of history, culture, and innovation.

CHAPTER 3

KYOTO'S CULTURAL HERITAGE

OVERVIEW OF KYOTO'S CULTURAL HERITAGE

Kyoto's cultural heritage stands as a testament to centuries of tradition, artistry, and spiritual devotion, earning the city UNESCO World Heritage status for its unparalleled collection of historical sites and cultural treasures.

Overview of Kyoto's Cultural Heritage

Temples and Shrines:

The city is adorned with over 1,600 temples and shrines, each steeped in history and architectural splendor. From the iconic Kinkaku-ji (Golden Pavilion) and Kiyomizu-dera's dramatic wooden stage to the serene beauty of Fushimi Inari Taisha's vermilion torii gates, these sacred sites epitomize spiritual devotion and architectural brilliance.

Traditional Arts and Crafts:

Kyoto is the birthplace of traditional Japanese arts and crafts. This area's artisans specialize in traditional crafts like tea ceremony utensils, Kyoto-style ceramics (Kyo-yaki), Nishijin weaving for kimono textiles, and exquisite Kyo-kumihimo braided cords. These crafts demonstrate the city's commitment to preserving traditional techniques passed down through generations.

Geisha Culture:

Its Gion district serves as a living museum of the geishan culture of Japan. Tourists are able to witness the skill and grace of geiko (geisha) and maiko(apprentice geisha) as they stroll through the atmospheric streets, preserving traditional entertainment, dance, music, and hospitality.

Traditional Festivals:

Kyoto's calendar is replete with historic and thrilling festivals like Gion Matsuri, Jidai Matsuri, and Aoi Matsuri. Featuring colorful parades, ancient customs, and ceremonial performances, these festivals offer a glimpse into Japan's rich cultural heritage.

Gardens and Zen Culture:

Zen culture is embodied in the city's well-designed gardens, including the serene Zen gardens of Ryoan-ji and the harmonious Saiho-ji (Kokedera) with its lush greenery. Amidst the splendor of nature, these quiet spaces invite contemplation and meditative immersion.

The cultural heritage of Kyoto is a mosaic with threads of tradition, spirituality, and artistic excellence. It functions as a museum that integrates ancient customs with modern life, offering visitors an opportunity to be immersed in a world where the resonance of history continues in the present, creating an unforgettable journey through Japan's cultural heritage.

TRADITIONAL ARTS AND CRAFTS OF KYOTO

Craftsmanship in Ceramics (Kyo-yaki):

Kyoto's legacy in ceramics, known as Kyo-yaki, spans centuries, embodying meticulous artistry and refined aesthetics. Artisans employ traditional techniques to create exquisite pottery, often adorned with intricate designs and vibrant colors. From delicate tea sets to ornate vases, Kyo-yaki showcases the city's commitment to preserving and evolving its ceramic heritage.

Nishijin Weaving and Kimono Textiles:

Nishijin district is a well-known location for Kyoto's textile industry, which has been around for centuries, producing intricate fabrics for Japan's traditional clothing, particularly kimono. Nishijin weaving is a meticulous craft that utilizes a variety of weaving techniques to create intricate patterns and textures, often using gold and silver threads. In this region, the kimono textiles are not limited to clothing but can also be considered as tangible art pieces, thanks to Kyoto's emphasis on textile traditions.

Tea Ceremony Utensils (Chado):

Chado, also known as the art of tea ceremony, is closely linked to Kyoto's cultural heritage. Craftsmen are skilled in crafting tea ceremony utensils, such as tea bowls (chawan), tea caddies (natsume), and bamboo whisks (chasen). The simplicity and elegance of these pieces are essential to the spiritual and aesthetic aspects of the traditional tea ceremony.

Kyoto-style Lacquerware (Kyo-shikki):

Kyoto's lacquerware, Kyo-shikki, demonstrates the city's skill in crafting lacquered creations. With great skill, artisans add multiple layers of lacquer to wood or other materials and create intricate designs or delicate mother-of-pearl inlays. A stunning collection of lacquered items, ranging from tableware to decorative boxes, has been produced, revered for their beauty and durability.

Bamboo Crafts (Takezaiku):

Takezaiku craftsmen, who are Kyoto artisans known for their use of bamboo in various forms, produce a vast range of products using this versatile material. By utilizing bamboo as a raw material for baskets, utensils, and art pieces, these craftsmen showcase Kyoto's modern approach to traditional craft.

Many of Kyoto's traditional arts and crafts are more than just art objects; they are living examples of the city's commitment to conserving its cultural heritage. With these artisans preserving traditional techniques and artistic excellence, Kyoto remains an active hub where ancient traditions coexist with modern life, providing visitors with a glimpse into Japan's rich artistic heritage.

KYOTO'S GEISHA CULTURE

Preserving an Ancient Tradition:

Kyoto stands as the epicenter of Japan's geisha culture, nurturing and preserving this centuries-old tradition. Geisha, known locally as geiko (women) and maiko (apprentices), are highly skilled entertainers trained in various traditional arts like dance, music, and conversation. The Gion and Pontocho districts serve as the focal points of Kyoto's geisha community, where these artisans uphold customs dating back to feudal Japan.

Training and Apprenticeship:

Becoming a geisha involves years of rigorous training. The apprenticeship of young girls who want to become maiko involves learning traditional arts, mastering intricate dance forms, playing musical instruments like the shamisen, and mastering conversation and hospitality skills. This is the culmination of years of dedicated practice and refinement, when one transitions from maiko to geiko.

Exquisite Attire and Graceful Artistry:

Geisha are known for their stunning attire, which includes intricate kimonos with elaborate obis (sashes), detailed hairstyles, and white makeup. Every aspect of their physical appearance holds cultural significance, with hair ornamentation and other accessories reflecting either the maiko's apprenticeship period or that of the geiki. Their polished gestures and graceful movements captivate audiences during performances and interactions.

Cultural Ambassadors and Entertainers:

As cultural ambassadors, Geisha provide a glimpse into Japan's traditional arts and customary traditions. They arrange events called ozashiki, where visitors can enjoy traditional entertainment, storytelling, games, and musical performances, all while immersing themselves in Kyoto's rich cultural heritage.

Preservation Efforts and Contemporary Relevance:

These efforts to preserve and promote the geisha culture have continued despite numbers declining over time. Other events, such as public performances and cultural showcases are intended to educate locals and tourists about the beauty of geisha traditions. Despite being steeped in tradition, Kyoto's geisha culture is still evolving, adapting to modern times while maintaining its traditional significance as an embodiment of Japan's cultural heritage.

Kyoto's geisha culture embodies grace, artistry, and a dedication to preserving Japan's historical traditions. Through their performances and presence, geisha continue to captivate audiences, offering a glimpse into a bygone era while maintaining an enduring legacy that enriches Kyoto's cultural landscape.

KYOTO'S TRADITIONAL FESTIVALS

Gion Matsuri:

Gion Matsuri stands as one of Japan's most iconic festivals, celebrated throughout July in honor of Yasaka Shrine. This month-long extravaganza dates back over a millennium, featuring vibrant processions known as Yamaboko Junko, where towering floats adorned with intricate tapestries parade through the city's streets. The festival culminates in the Yamaboko Junko Grand Parade on July 17th, drawing crowds to witness the spectacle of traditional music, dance, and cultural displays.

Jidai Matsuri:

In October, Kyoto hosts the Jidai Matsuri, the Festival of Ages. In this celebration of Kyoto's rich history, the city is paraded by people dressed in costumes from different periods during Kyoto's history. This impressive procession starts at the Imperial Palace and proceeds to Heian Shrine, offering a fascinating insight into Kyoto's cultural history from the past centuries.

Aoi Matsuri:

The Aoi Matsuri is a celebration held in May that involves a grand procession from Kyoto Imperial Palace to the Shimogamo and Kamigamo Shrines. Participants don Heian-era clothing from the past, highlighting their period splendor. Over 500 individuals, dressed in aristocratic attire and ceremonial outfits, were present, symbolizing the grandeur of Kyoto's history.

Hanatoro in Higashiyama:

Kyoto's Higashiyama district is illuminated in the brilliant daylight of Hanatoro in March. A stunning radiance is cast by lanterns that line the streets and temples, creating a mesmerizing aura over the ancient community. Guests can enjoy the magical nighttime scenery of the city's traditional architecture and cherry blossoms as they stroll along illuminated pathways.

Festival of Lanterns (Toro Nagashi):

In the middle of August, during the Toro Nagashi festival, lanterns are released onto the Kamo River to honor ancestral spirits and display their floating form. A tranquil and touching ceremony provides an opportunity for participants to write messages on lanterns before launching them onto the water, creating a peaceful atmosphere along the riverbanks.

The traditional festivals in Kyoto are full of history and offer visitors a unique chance to experience the city's rich cultural bounty. The festivals each represent a reflection of Kyoto's rich history, providing insights into ancient customs, rituals, and artistic traditions that persist in the city's modern atmosphere.

CHAPTER 4

TOP DESTINATIONS IN KYOTO AND WHAT TO DO

KINKAKU-JI (GOLDEN PAVILION)

What's Popular About It:

Kinkaku-ji, or the Golden Pavilion, is a shimmering symbol of beauty and tranquility. The top two floors of this Zen Buddhist temple are covered in gold leaf, reflecting majestically on the pond that surrounds it. The architectural splendor, juxtaposed against the serene landscape, creates a breathtaking sight.

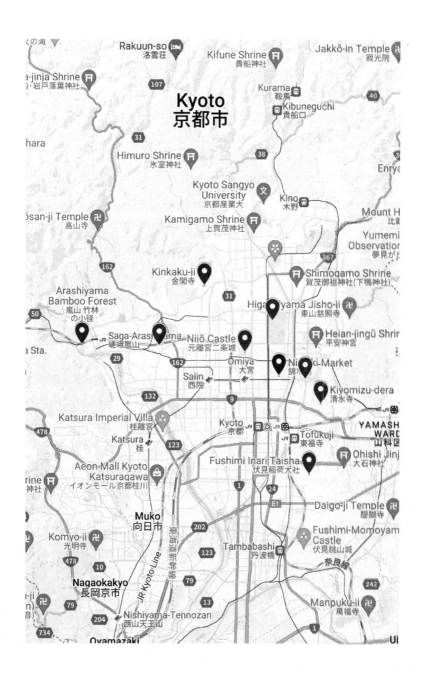

https://www.google.com/maps/d/edit?mid=1FbDPuM8ZK
MlHJ1SonOoTBVFrS0wt0X0&ll=35.01577546491987%2
C135.73881504063806&z=16

Why You Shouldn't Miss It:

This magnificent temple in Kyoto is a must to see. But the sheer magnificence of this Golden Pavilion against the carefully landscaped garden is so stunning, you can't help but wonder where you are headed next. This serene sanctuary is an embodiment of Zen philosophy and its historical relevance.

Best Time to Get There:

Early morning or late afternoon is the most suitable time to visit the Golden Pavilion and enjoy it with fewer crowds. Kinkaku-ji is a serene location with an attractive garden and impressive architecture, regardless of the time.

Location:

The northern part of Kyoto is where Kinkaku-ji is located, and it is easily accessible with public transportation options such as bus routes 101 or 205. It's nestled amidst lush greenery, providing a serene escape from the city's bustle.

Helpful Insider Tips:

Just come in, early morning -- this will be quieter and more contemplative than arriving at the temple earlier. Take note of the reflection of the pavilion in the pond; it's truly captivating. In addition, a trip in autumn offers an extra special treat, as the leaves change into a colorful mosaic.

Insider Advice:

While there are no special conditions for visiting Kinkaku-ji, it is important to keep in mind that certain areas may be closed to the public. Obtaining either a guidebook or audio guide is the way to fully grasp this famous temple's history and culture.

Known for its beauty and spiritual tranquility, Kinkaku-ji is the epitome of Kyoto's charm and serenity. The sight of its sparkling gold against the backdrop of nature is a visual treat that tugs at the heartstrings of those who come in.

FUSHIMI INARI TAISHA

Located in southern Kyoto, Fushimi Inari Taisha is an iconic Shinto shrine renowned for its thousands of vibrant orange torii gates that form mesmerizing pathways through the forested Mount Inari. This sacred site is dedicated to Inari, the Shinto god of rice and prosperity, making it a revered destination for prayers related to success and good fortune.

The picturesque trails lined with torii gates that wind their way up the mountain are what make Fushimi Inari Taisha truly unforgettable. Each gate, which has been donated by individuals and businesses, bears the donor's name and represents a wish or offering. The hike to the summit, which includes several smaller shrines and panoramic views of Kyoto, takes approximately 2-3 hours.

To avoid crowds, visit early in the morning or late in the afternoon, especially on weekends or during peak tourist seasons. However, regardless of the season, the allure of Fushimi Inari Taisha lies in exploring its trails, taking in the tranquil atmosphere, and watching the play of light and shadow amidst the gates.

The shrine is easily accessible via a short train ride from Kyoto Station to Fushimi Inari Station. Insider tip: Consider arriving early to enjoy the peace and quiet on the quieter trails. Wear comfortable hiking shoes and bring water, especially during the warmer months.

There are no special requirements to visit, but due to the uphill climb, exploring the trails requires a moderate level of fitness. In addition, if you're curious about the shrine's history and significance, a guidebook or an audio guide can provide useful information during your visit.

Fushimi Inari Taisha is not just a shrine; it's a spiritual journey through a mesmerizing landscape of gates, woods, and cultural significance. It offers a unique experience that unveils the spiritual fabric of Kyoto while providing breathtaking views and moments of reflection amidst nature.

ARASHIYAMA BAMBOO GROVE

Nestled in the western outskirts of Kyoto, the Arashiyama Bamboo Grove stands as a natural wonder and cultural gem. This enchanting bamboo forest, known for its towering stalks that create a serene, almost otherworldly atmosphere, offers a unique and immersive experience for visitors.

The awe-inspiring landscape draws visitors here, where sunlight filters through the densely packed bamboo stalks, casting ethereal patterns of light and shadow along the forest pathways. The tranquil atmosphere created by the swaying bamboo creates a tranquil escape from the urban hustle, making it a must-see destination in Kyoto.

To enjoy the beauty of the Bamboo Grove without the crowds, go early in the morning or late in the afternoon. Its proximity to other Arashiyama attractions, such as nearby temples and the iconic Togetsukyo Bridge, makes it an ideal addition to a day of sightseeing.

The Bamboo Grove is conveniently located within walking distance of Arashiyama Station. Insider tip: Arrive early to enjoy the tranquil atmosphere and take stunning photos away from the crowds. Consider venturing beyond the main path for a more peaceful experience.

There are no special requirements to visit the Bamboo Grove, but it is recommended that you wear comfortable shoes for walking and exploring the trails. Furthermore, visiting during the weekdays or early mornings provides a more tranquil encounter with the enthralling bamboo forest.

The Arashiyama Bamboo Grove is a natural wonder that showcases the tranquil beauty of Kyoto's natural landscapes. The gentle rustling of bamboo leaves and the play of light through the dense grove create an immersive and unforgettable experience for all who visit.

KIYOMIZU-DERA

Perched on the eastern hills of Kyoto, Kiyomizu-dera, or the "Pure Water Temple," is a UNESCO World Heritage Site that epitomizes both architectural beauty and spiritual significance. This iconic temple, dating back to the 8th century, commands breathtaking views of Kyoto from its wooden veranda, offering visitors an awe-inspiring panorama.

The striking main hall, built entirely without nails and displaying the architectural mastery of ancient craftsmen, is what makes Kiyomizu-dera an unmissable destination. The wooden veranda, which juts out from the hillside, offers stunning views of cherry blossoms in spring and fiery foliage in autumn, making it a photographer's dream.

The best time to visit is during the cherry blossom season in spring or the autumn foliage, but the temple's allure remains enchanting all year. Early morning visits are recommended to avoid crowds.

Kiyomizu-dera is located in the historic Higashiyama district and is easily accessible by bus or a scenic walk from Kyoto Station. Before entering the main hall, perform the temple's ritual of drinking from the Otowa Waterfall for health, longevity, or success. Explore the charming traditional shops and cafes that line the streets leading up to the temple.

There are no special requirements for visiting, but comfortable shoes are recommended due to the incline of the temple grounds. A guidebook or audio guide can also enhance the experience by providing information about the temple's history and cultural significance.

Kiyomizu-dera is a testament to Kyoto's spiritual and cultural heritage as well as an architectural marvel. Its commanding views, combined with its tranquil ambiance and rich history, create an immersive experience that captivates every visitor's soul.

GION DISTRICT

Nestled in the heart of Kyoto, the Gion district exudes an enchanting ambiance steeped in tradition, making it a cultural haven revered for its geisha heritage and preserved historical charm.

Gion's reputation as the pinnacle of Kyoto's geisha culture draws visitors. While strolling through the atmospheric streets, one can catch glimpses of geiko and maiko gracefully making their way to appointments, their vibrant kimonos and elaborate hairstyles adding radiance to the surroundings. Witnessing their performances or taking part in an ozashiki (traditional entertainment gathering) provides an immersive experience into this time-honored tradition.

Early evening is the best time to visit Gion because the district comes alive with an air of elegance and mystique. Visitors can stroll through the streets lined with traditional wooden machiya houses, taking in the tranquil beauty of lantern-lit pathways and the Shirakawa Stream.

Gion is easily accessible, being located within walking distance of major attractions such as Kiyomizu-dera and Yasaka Shrine. Insider tip: While exploring, go to Hanami-koji, one of Gion's historic streets, to see geisha in their element. Consider stopping by the Gion Corner for a curated display of traditional arts.

There are no special requirements to visit Gion, but it is recommended that you respect the district's cultural significance. Consider taking a guided tour or seeing a cultural show to learn more about Gion's geisha culture and history.

Gion's allure stems not only from its aesthetic appeal, but also from its ability to transport visitors to a bygone era, where tradition, elegance, and grace blend seamlessly with Kyoto's contemporary landscape. It is a living testament to Japan's rich cultural heritage, which continues to fascinate and enchant visitors from all over the world.

NIJO CASTLE

Embracing centuries of history and architectural grandeur, Nijo Castle stands as a symbol of power and refinement in the heart of Kyoto. This UNESCO World Heritage Site transports visitors back to Japan's feudal era, offering a glimpse into the country's historical legacy.

The magnificent architecture of Nijo Castle, including the opulent Ninomaru Palace, makes it a must-see. This palace, known for its "nightingale floors" that chirp when walked on, served as the residence for shoguns and nobles, and was lavishly decorated with intricate paintings and exquisite craftsmanship.

To avoid crowds, visit Nijo Castle during the weekdays or early in the morning. A captivating experience is strolling through the castle's meticulously landscaped gardens and viewing the ornate interiors.

Nijo Castle is located near central Kyoto and is easily accessible by public transportation. Insider tip: Consider taking a guided tour to learn more about the castle's history and architectural significance. Don't miss out on the garden's seasonal displays, especially the cherry blossoms in spring and the vibrant foliage in autumn.

Nijo Castle has no special requirements, but comfortable footwear is recommended for exploring the expansive grounds. Using audio guides or guidebooks can help you better understand the castle's historical and cultural significance.

Nijo Castle is a testament to Japan's feudal past, providing a glimpse into the Edo period's opulence, power, and artistry. Its grandeur and historical significance make it an unmissable destination, inviting visitors to immerse themselves in the rich cultural tapestry that is Kyoto.

KYOTO IMPERIAL PALACE

At the heart of Kyoto lies the Kyoto Imperial Palace, a tangible link to Japan's imperial history and a revered symbol of the country's monarchy.

The Imperial Palace's historical significance as the former residence of Japan's imperial family draws visitors. The sprawling grounds, surrounded by moats and walls, house a variety of halls, gardens, and meticulously preserved buildings that once served as the seat of political power.

The best time to visit the Imperial Palace is during guided tours, which are available multiple times per day except on Sundays and holidays. These guided tours provide access to the palace's inner sanctums as well as insights into Japan's imperial history, traditions, and architectural styles.

The Imperial Palace is easily accessible by public transportation because it is located near Kyoto Station. Insider tip: Guided tours require advance reservations, which can be made through the Imperial Household Agency's website. Consider going to the nearby Sento Imperial Palace, which requires separate reservations but provides a more intimate look at imperial architecture and gardens.

There are specific guidelines for visiting the Imperial Palace, such as dress codes and area restrictions. Follow these guidelines to respect the cultural significance of the palace and to ensure its preservation.

The Kyoto Imperial Palace provides a rare glimpse into Japan's imperial past, inviting visitors to immerse themselves in a world of history, tradition, and regal elegance. It is a place where the legacy of Japan's monarchy is preserved and shared with those interested in the country's history.

NISHIKI MARKET

Nestled in the heart of Kyoto, Nishiki Market stands as a vibrant culinary haven, celebrated for its rich array of traditional foods, local delicacies, and bustling atmosphere.

The extensive selection of fresh produce, seafood, sweets, and specialty goods at Nishiki Market makes it a must-visit. The five-block-long covered arcade houses over a hundred shops and stalls, each offering a unique gastronomic experience. The market embodies Kyoto's culinary heritage, offering everything from pickled vegetables and fresh seafood to matcha-flavored delights and traditional sweets.

The best time to visit Nishiki Market is in the morning or early afternoon, when the market is busy and the freshest produce is available. Engaging with local vendors, sampling various flavors, and learning about Kyoto's traditional ingredients provide an immersive cultural experience.

Nishiki Market is a short walk from Shijo Station and is centrally located and easily accessible from major attractions.

Insider tip: Come hungry and look for hidden gems in the less-traveled alleys. Consider buying local specialties like tsukemono (pickles) or yuba (tofu skin) to get a taste of the authentic Kyoto flavors.

There are no special requirements to visit Nishiki Market, but bring cash because some vendors may not accept credit cards. Bringing a reusable bag for any purchases is also convenient and environmentally friendly.

Nishiki Market is a culinary adventure waiting to be discovered, taking visitors on a sensory journey through Kyoto's diverse flavors and food culture. It's a gathering place for locals and visitors alike to savor the essence of Kyoto's gastronomic treasures.

TOEI KYOTO STUDIO PARK

Nestled on the outskirts of Kyoto, Toei Kyoto Studio Park is a captivating destination that seamlessly blends entertainment, history, and culture, offering visitors a glimpse into Japan's cinematic past and present.

The immersive experience in Edo-period Japan makes Toei Kyoto Studio Park an appealing stop. The park includes a recreated Edo-era town with period-style buildings, streets, and theatrical performances. Visitors can watch live ninja shows and samurai sword fights, as well as dress up in traditional costumes, for an interactive journey through Japan's feudal era.

To avoid crowds and fully enjoy the park's various performances and attractions, visit during the weekdays. Exploring the intricately designed sets, engaging with the interactive exhibits, and participating in theatrical shows provide an entertaining and educational experience.

Toei Kyoto Studio Park is conveniently located near central Kyoto and is easily accessible by public transportation. Insider tip: Attend the park's special events, which frequently include behind-the-scenes tours, workshops, and one-of-a-kind performances. Also, look for opportunities to participate in costume rentals for a more immersive experience.

There are no special requirements for visiting the park, but because it involves walking, comfortable footwear is recommended. Engaging with the interactive elements and performances also improves the overall experience.

Toei Kyoto Studio Park provides an exciting blend of entertainment and history, transporting visitors back in time to experience Japan's Edo period's vibrant culture and excitement. It's a one-of-a-kind destination that combines cinematic artistry and historical reenactments to captivate audiences of all ages.

CHAPTER 5

KYOTO'S TEMPLES AND SHRINES

OVERVIEW OF KYOTO'S TEMPLES AND SHRINES

Kyoto, a city steeped in spiritual devotion and historical significance, is a treasure trove of temples and shrines that weave a tapestry of Japan's rich cultural heritage. As you wander through its streets, you'll find yourself immersed in a landscape adorned with countless sacred sites, each possessing its own unique allure and historical resonance.

A Haven of Spiritual Sanctuaries:
From grandiose temples to intimate shrines, Kyoto's urban landscape is graced by these timeless monuments. The city boasts over 1,600 Buddhist temples and Shinto shrines, making it a haven for spiritual exploration and cultural immersion.

A Glimpse into Japan's Spiritual Essence:

The temples and shrines in Kyoto provide a glimpse into Japan's spiritual heritage. Each of these sites represents a chapter in the religious and cultural development of the nation; it is an example of architectural brilliance, ornate structures of intricate scales, and a reverence for tradition.

A Tapestry of Architectural Marvels:

The architectural style of Kyoto's temples and shrines is a fascinating blend of features, encompassing the grand architecture of Heian-era buildings and the unassuming elegance of Zen-inspired designs. Sculpture: The ornate detailing, serene gardens and the natural balance between man-made architecture and its surroundings creates a sense of peace and calm.

A Spiritual Journey Amidst Nature:

A significant portion of Kyoto's temples and shrines are located in lush gardens or on the hillsides, providing visitors with a sense of spiritual serenity amidst stunning natural scenery.

A Blend of Past and Present:

Although steeped in history, these sites are still living cultural landmarks, often hosting festivals and ceremonies that provide insight into the long-standing traditions of Japan.

Kyoto's temples and shrines stand as guardians of the city's soul, inviting travelers to embark on a spiritual odyssey through Japan's historical and religious heritage. Visiting these sacred areas as you traverse Kyoto's streets will reveal the heart of a culture steeped in tradition, reverence, and spiritual enlightenment.

MUST-SEE TEMPLES IN KYOTO

Kinkaku-ji (Golden Pavilion)

An iconic symbol of Kyoto, Kinkaku-ji mesmerizes with its golden exterior set against a reflective pond and serene gardens. The temple's dazzling beauty, especially during sunrise or sunset, is truly captivating. Located in northern Kyoto, this temple's allure lies in its striking architecture and the way its golden façade shimmers in the surrounding landscape. It's a must-visit for its breathtaking aesthetic and serene ambiance.

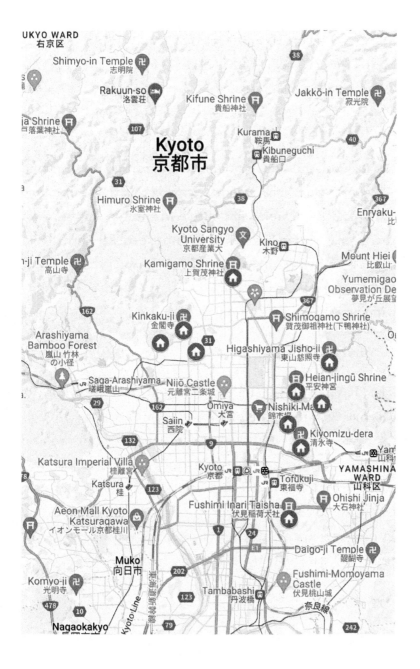

https://www.google.com/maps/d/edit?mid=1FbDPuM8ZK
MlHJ1SonOoTBVFrS0wt0X0&ll=35.038311529901165%2
C135.74089729985934&z=14

Kiyomizu-dera

Located on a hillside, Kiyomizu-dera provides breathtaking views of Kyoto. The wooden veranda, offering panoramic vistas, and the temple's impressive architecture and seasonal charm, make it a quintessential Kyoto experience. Situated in the east of Kyoto, this temple is famous for its magnificent views and grand architectural design. It's worth a visit for its panoramic views and cultural value.

Fushimi Inari Taisha

The Fushimi Inari Taisha, which is renowned for its captivating pathways adorned with thousands of vermilion torii gates, offers visitors a glimpse into an exotic wooded landscape situated on Mount Inari. At this shrine dedicated to Inari, you will find serene trails and stunning views. In southern Kyoto, the shrine's torii gates make for an intriguing journey through nature. A must-see with its scenic and immersive trails.

Ryoan-ji

The Zen rock garden at Ryoan-ji is a place where simplicity meets serenity. In a peaceful setting, the rock garden's minimalist design invites reflection and contemplation. Positioned in the northwest of Kyoto, this temple's serene rock garden is a popular spot for taking in the stillness of nature. It's the ultimate destination for those seeking a peaceful and deliberate experience.

Ginkaku-ji (Silver Pavilion)

Despite its lack of real silver embellishments, Ginkaku-ji's peaceful gardens are still beautifully designed and well-groomed. It's a peaceful place, with subtle elegance and the surrounding moss gardens. It is located on Kyoto's eastern hills and is famous for its tranquil gardens with a subdued atmosphere. It's worth visiting for its peaceful setting and beautifully designed surroundings.

Nanzen-ji

A grand temple complex with awe-inspiring gardens, Nanzen-ji is home to impressive structures like Sanmon Gate and Hojo Hall. Both the serene stone garden and its aqueduct bridge are alluring to visitors. The grandeur of Nanzen-ji, situated in the eastern part of Kyoto, is due to its vast grounds and impressive historical structures. It's worth visiting for its culturally rich and peaceful vibe.

Byodo-in

Located in Uji, a short trip from Kyoto, Byodo-in's Phoenix Hall is an architectural gem and a UNESCO World Heritage Site. The hall's symmetrical beauty and tranquil surroundings make it a must-visit. Situated in nearby Uji, Byodo-in's attraction is its UNESCO-listed Phoenix Hall.

It's a must-visit for its historical significance and captivating beauty.

MUST-SEE SHRINES IN KYOTO

Fushimi Inari Taisha is renowned for its thousands of vibrant torii gates creating a mesmerizing path ascending Mount Inari in southern Kyoto. Visitors are enchanted by the immersive experience wandering through serene forests, offering picturesque views of the city. Situated at the base of Mount Inari, its spiritual aura dedicated to Inari beckons with unique trails, making it an essential and captivating attraction.

Yasaka Shrine, also known as Gion Shrine, enchants visitors with its vibrant festivals, especially the iconic Gion Matsuri, which takes place in July. The lantern-lit paths and festive ambiance of the shrine create an enchanting atmosphere. Yasaka Shrine, located in central Kyoto's Gion district, is historically significant and serves as a cultural hub, inviting visitors for a rich cultural experience beyond its renowned festivals.

Heian Shrine is notable for its massive torii gate and sprawling vermilion architecture set amidst a spacious garden that provides visitors with tranquillity. Its impressive design and seasonal allure, especially during cherry blossom season, provide a cultural and historical glimpse of Kyoto's heritage. It is located in eastern Kyoto near the Philosopher's Path.

Kamigamo Shrine and Shimogamo Shrine, known collectively as "Kamo-san," are UNESCO World Heritage Sites steeped in ancient Shinto traditions. These tranquil shrines in northern Kyoto's forested areas welcome visitors seeking spiritual solace and cultural enlightenment, with unique rituals and peaceful natural settings.

Kitano Tenmangu Shrine, located northwest of central Kyoto, is known for its seasonal beauty, hosting plum blossom festivals in the spring and vibrant foliage displays in the autumn. The shrine's historical significance, cultural events, and bustling markets provide a distinct cultural experience beyond its natural allure. It is dedicated to Tenjin, the deity of scholarship.

Each of these shrines in Kyoto encapsulates unique facets of Japanese culture, spirituality, and tradition, inviting travelers to explore their historical significance, immerse themselves in vibrant festivals, and find solace in the tranquility of these sacred sites.

HIDDEN GEMS: LESSER-KNOWN TEMPLES AND SHRINES

Jingo-ji Temple: Tucked away in the Takao mountains, Jingo-ji Temple offers a tranquil escape from the city's hustle. Its secluded setting allows visitors to explore serene trails amid lush forests. The main hall's rustic charm and the panoramic view of Kyoto from the observation deck make this temple a hidden delight.

Joju-in Temple: Nestled near Nanzen-ji, Joju-in Temple captivates with its captivating stone garden, offering a serene ambiance for contemplation. Visitors can appreciate the garden's intricate designs and the temple's intimate setting, providing a peaceful retreat away from crowds.

Raigo-in Temple: Raigo-in Temple, located on Mount Myoho, is a hidden gem that is known for its breathtaking autumn foliage. The vibrant maple trees and tranquil atmosphere of the temple provide a picturesque setting for nature enthusiasts and photographers.

Kurama-dera: Located in the northern mountains, Kurama-dera exudes mystical charm. The temple's lush surroundings and the hike up through forested trails offer a sense of spiritual awakening. The onsen experience and the annual Kurama Fire Festival add to its allure.

Kaju-ji Temple: Kaju-ji Temple, located near Takao, entices visitors with its tranquil pond garden and historical structures. The temple's lesser-known status ensures a peaceful visit, allowing visitors to appreciate the temple's quiet beauty and ancient artifacts.

Manshu-in Temple: Hidden in the quieter Higashiyama district, Manshu-in Temple features exquisite sliding door paintings and serene rock gardens. The temple's refined elegance and the peaceful surroundings offer a serene retreat for those seeking cultural and artistic delights.

These lesser-known temples and shrines reveal hidden treasures and tranquil havens, making them ideal for travelers looking for a more intimate and authentic experience of Kyoto's rich spiritual heritage and natural beauty. Exploring these hidden gems away from the crowds allows for a deeper connection with Kyoto's cultural tapestry, providing moments of tranquility and discovery.

CHAPTER 6

KYOTO'S GARDENS AND PARKS

OVERVIEW OF KYOTO'S GARDENS AND PARKS

Kyoto, a city revered for its cultural richness, isn't just a canvas of ancient temples and historical landmarks—it's a landscape adorned with an array of meticulously crafted gardens and serene parks. These green spaces, scattered throughout the city, embody the soul of Kyoto, showcasing the Japanese penchant for nature and design.

A garden or park awaits in almost every corner of Kyoto, each with its own story and allure. Kyoto's green havens offer an intimate connection to nature and a glimpse into Japan's aesthetic principles, from the poetic elegance of Katsura Imperial Villa's meticulously planned landscapes to the tranquil hideaways in Okochi Sanso Garden.

The city has an impressive collection of gardens, some attached to imperial villas and others integrated with historic sites, that invite visitors to stroll through verdant paths, pause by tranquil ponds, and admire meticulously manicured landscapes. These aren't just flower displays; they're living works of art that embody meticulous design philosophies and historical legacies.

Parks, too, dot the cityscape, providing pockets of respite amidst the chaos. The Kyoto Imperial Palace Park, which surrounds the Imperial Palace, features expansive open spaces and elegant gardens steeped in regal history. Meanwhile, during the spring, Maruyama Park transforms into a canvas of pink hues, inviting locals and visitors alike to partake in the cherished tradition of hanami.

Each of these spaces, from the historic Nijo Castle Gardens to the contemplative Ryoan-ji Temple's Stone Garden, tells a story—a story of cultural heritage, aesthetic refinement, and a deep reverence for nature. Their tranquil settings invite reflection, their seasonal blooms provide visual feasts, and their historical ties provide glimpses into Kyoto's rich history.

To truly experience Kyoto's essence, venture beyond its bustling streets and temples and into the tranquillity of its gardens and parks. They are more than just tourist attractions; they are living testaments to the intricate relationship that the Japanese people have with the natural world—an essential part of the tapestry that makes Kyoto an enduring cultural gem.

MUST-SEE GARDENS IN KYOTO

Katsura Imperial Villa Gardens: Tucked away in western Kyoto, the Katsura Imperial Villa Gardens embody unparalleled beauty and meticulous design. These gardens, part of the Imperial Family's villa, harmoniously blend nature with architectural brilliance. Every feature, from the serene ponds reflecting perfectly pruned trees to the carefully crafted pathways, showcases the essence of Japanese aesthetics. Visitors need advance reservations for guided tours, allowing an insightful glimpse into Japan's aristocratic heritage and the subtle intricacies of garden design, making this experience a true gem.

Okochi Sanso Garden: The Okochi Sanso Garden, which is part of actor Denjiro Okochi's former villa and is embraced by the tranquility of the Arashiyama district, beckons with

enchanting landscapes. This garden weaves bamboo groves, trickling streams, and scenic viewpoints together, each revealing the beauty of nature. The admission price includes matcha tea, which guests can savor while admiring the panoramic views of Kyoto. A visit here provides not only natural beauty but also a tranquil retreat away from the crowds, ideal for quiet contemplation and appreciation of nature's artistry.

Ryoan-ji Temple's Stone Garden: Ryoan-ji Temple's Stone Garden in northwest Kyoto is revered as a quintessential Zen rock garden that transcends simplicity into profound beauty. Its fifteen carefully placed rocks amidst raked gravel elicit introspection and contemplation. Visitors who seek tranquillity and philosophical insights are frequently engrossed in deciphering the garden's enigmatic arrangement. Early mornings and late afternoons provide quieter times for a more immersive experience in this temple's serene setting.

Nijo Castle Gardens: The Nijo Castle Gardens, located within the historic Nijo Castle, exude elegance and historical significance. These gardens, which feature meticulously landscaped ponds, vibrant flora, and majestic pine trees, complement the grandeur of the castle. Visitors exploring the castle's interior can unwind in these tranquil gardens, which are stunning in all seasons. A visit in the early morning or late afternoon allows for a tranquil stroll through the lush landscapes, providing a welcome respite.

Maruyama Park: Located near Yasaka Shrine in central Kyoto, Maruyama Park comes alive during cherry blossom season. Its massive weeping cherry tree, which is illuminated at night, serves as the focal point of hanami gatherings. Locals and visitors alike gather to celebrate this cherished tradition, picnicking beneath the canopy of blossoms. Arriving early in the morning or late in the evening creates a more intimate atmosphere among nature's ephemeral beauty.

Each of these gardens in Kyoto encapsulates distinct facets of Japanese aesthetics, offering serene retreats, cultural insights, and a profound connection with nature. Exploring these spaces reveals not just beauty but narratives of history, artistry, and the intricate relationship between human creation and the natural world.

MUST-SEE PARKS IN KYOTO

Kyoto Imperial Palace Park: Encompassing the Kyoto Imperial Palace, this park boasts vast open spaces, elegant gardens, and historical significance. Visitors can explore the palace's extensive grounds and serene landscapes while learning about Kyoto's imperial history through guided tours. Early morning visits offer tranquil moments amidst the peaceful surroundings before the crowds arrive. The park provides a serene oasis in the heart of the city, inviting contemplation and a deeper appreciation for Kyoto's regal past.

Arashiyama Bamboo Grove: The Arashiyama Bamboo Grove in western Kyoto, while not a traditional park, provides an enchanting natural spectacle. With filtered sunlight casting ethereal shadows, the towering bamboo stalks create a captivating path. Arriving early in the morning or late in the afternoon allows for a more peaceful experience, allowing visitors to enjoy the serene ambiance and capture the grove's tranquil beauty without the hustle and bustle of the crowds.

Umekoji Park: Umekoji Park, located near Kyoto Station, provides a peaceful respite from the city's bustle. This expansive park features open lawns, walking paths, and a picturesque pond, making it a relaxing setting for picnics, leisurely strolls, or simply unwinding among nature's serenity. The tranquillity of the park makes it an ideal spot for a casual retreat or a brief respite while exploring Kyoto's bustling urban areas.

Higashi Park: Higashi Park, located near Higashi Hongan-ji Temple, enchants visitors with its simplicity and peaceful ambiance. This lesser-known park has a beautifully manicured Japanese garden that provides a tranquil setting for meditation and relaxation. Its proximity to the temple allows for a peaceful walk that combines cultural exploration with quiet contemplation.

Tetsugaku no Michi (Philosopher's Path): Though not a traditional park, this picturesque canal-side path in Kyoto's northern outskirts provides a delightful mix of nature and culture. The path is lined with cherry trees that bloom in the spring and is ideal for contemplative strolls. Early morning or weekday visits provide a more solitary experience, providing a serene retreat and the opportunity to immerse oneself in the tranquil surroundings.

Each of these Kyoto parks offers a distinct experience, whether it's exploring historical landscapes, indulging in nature's beauty, or finding pockets of tranquility amid the city's bustle. From imperial splendor to tranquil bamboo groves, these spaces invite visitors to embrace Kyoto's many facets, providing moments of serenity and cultural immersion.

HIDDEN GEMS: LESSER-KNOWN GARDENS AND PARKS

Nestled amidst Kyoto's rich tapestry of renowned gardens and parks lie hidden sanctuaries that whisper tales of serenity and beauty—lesser-known yet equally enchanting spaces waiting to be discovered. These hidden gems, often overshadowed by their more famous counterparts, offer intimate retreats into nature's artistry and cultural heritage. Amidst Kyoto's bustling streets and acclaimed attractions, these hidden treasures invite seekers of quietude and cultural richness to unearth the nuanced beauty woven into their serene landscapes, promising intimate encounters with nature's splendor and historical significance.

Murin-an Garden: Murin-an Garden, located in the Higashiyama district, exudes a tranquil ambiance amidst lush greenery and serene landscapes. Jihei Ogawa's hidden gem offers an exquisite blend of traditional Japanese garden elements and modern landscaping techniques. Visitors can enjoy the garden's tranquil atmosphere while exploring its winding paths, gentle streams, and meticulously manicured foliage. Special tea events and guided tours offer more information about the garden's design and historical significance.

Yoshikien Garden: Yoshikien Garden, located near Nara-koen Park, is a collection of three distinct gardens: a tea garden, a moss garden, and a pond garden, each with its own distinct charm. Despite its proximity to popular attractions, this garden remains a tranquil haven, providing visitors with a peaceful escape. While immersed in the garden's serene ambiance, guests can appreciate the subtle beauty of moss-covered landscapes, vibrant seasonal blooms, and peaceful tea ceremonies.

Genko-an Temple's Moss Garden: Often overshadowed by larger attractions, the Moss Garden at Genko-an Temple in northern Kyoto is a hidden treasure. This small yet captivating garden features a sea of lush moss covering the ground, creating a serene and ethereal setting. Visitors can sit in contemplation within the temple hall, gazing at the moss garden through a small square window, a meditative experience known as the "Window of Enlightenment."

Kyoto Botanical Garden: The Kyoto Botanical Garden, located near Kitayama Station, offers a diverse collection of flora and expansive landscapes while remaining off the beaten path for many tourists. The garden features a diverse collection of plants from around the world, including a tranquil Japanese garden and extensive greenhouse collections. Visitors can take leisurely strolls through seasonal blooms and themed gardens for a full botanical experience.

Myoren-ji Temple Garden: Myoren-ji Temple, located in the western part of Kyoto, has a small but charming garden. The garden exudes tranquillity with its beautiful stone arrangements, moss-covered stones, and seasonal flora. Visitors can appreciate the garden's simplicity as well as the temple's serene atmosphere, which provides a peaceful respite from the city's bustle.

Kyoto's lesser-known gardens and parks contain hidden treasures just waiting to be discovered. Each embodies distinct aesthetics, cultural significance, and tranquil landscapes, offering visitors intimate and immersive experiences away from the crowds, making them delightful discoveries for those seeking tranquillity and hidden beauty in Kyoto.

CHAPTER 7

KYOTO'S MUSEUMS AND GALLERIES

OVERVIEW OF KYOTO'S MUSEUMS AND GALLERIES

Kyoto boasts a captivating array of museums and galleries that weave together the city's rich historical tapestry and artistic brilliance. From traditional art and history museums to modern art galleries, these cultural institutions are sprinkled throughout Kyoto, offering visitors an immersive journey into the city's heritage.

Aside from preserving Kyoto's history, these spaces serve as vibrant hubs, fostering social connections and cultural dialogues among locals and international visitors. Economically, they are critical in attracting tourists, scholars, and art enthusiasts, significantly contributing to Kyoto's thriving tourism industry. These museums engage with local communities through events, workshops, and educational programs, becoming integral parts of Kyoto's social fabric.

Through their exhibitions and advocacy for cultural preservation, these institutions subtly influence the city's political landscape. Collectively, Kyoto's museums and galleries stand not just as repositories of history and art but as dynamic spaces that animate the city's cultural vitality.

MUST-SEE MUSEUMS IN KYOTO

Kyoto National Museum: A cultural gem nestled in Higashiyama, this museum is a treasure trove of Japanese art and history. It's a perfect window into Kyoto's rich past, showcasing exquisite samurai armor, ancient scrolls, and traditional crafts. Pro tip: Don't miss their special exhibitions—they often feature rare artifacts not regularly on display.

Kyoto International Manga Museum: This museum is a haven for manga fans and curious visitors alike. It's more than just a place to read manga; it's a vibrant space dedicated to this unique art form. Insider tip: The extensive manga library is a treasure trove, and there are drawing workshops where you can let your inner artist loose.

Toei Kyoto Studio Park: This is a must-see for anyone interested in Japan's cinematic history. It's a theme park as well as a working studio where you can watch live-action samurai dramas and even dress up in period costumes. Insider tip: Arrive early to witness the filming—it's an immersive experience!

The Museum of Kyoto: This museum, hidden near Nijo Castle, delves deep into the city's history, showcasing its cultural evolution through the ages. Don't miss the exhibits that depict Kyoto's evolution over time. Check their calendar for special events; they frequently host talks and cultural performances.

Kyoto Railway Museum: Train enthusiasts and families adore this museum, exploring Japan's railway history through interactive exhibits and beautifully restored locomotives. Insider's tip: The simulator lets you experience driving a train—quite a thrilling experience!

Raku Museum: This unassuming gem in northern Kyoto honors the revered Raku pottery. It's a tranquil setting where you can admire the fine craftsmanship and learn more about this revered art form. Insider knowledge: Engage with the staff; they frequently share fascinating stories about the pottery.

These museums provide one-of-a-kind glimpses into Kyoto's diverse cultural heritage. Whether you're interested in traditional arts, manga culture, or film history, each museum will broaden your understanding of Kyoto's past and present. Check for special events and exhibitions to enhance your experience!

MUST-SEE GALLERIES IN KYOTO

Gallery Maronie: Tucked away in the artistic district of Gion, this gallery is a hidden gem showcasing contemporary Japanese art. The rotating exhibits feature diverse styles and emerging artists. Insider tip: Engage with the curator—they offer unique insights into the artists and their inspirations.

Kyoto Art Center: A hub for avant-garde art, this center in Shimogyo hosts innovative exhibitions and artist-in-residence programs. Don't miss their experimental showcases that challenge conventional artistic boundaries. Insider advice: Attend their workshops and talks for a deeper understanding of contemporary art practices.

Museum of Contemporary Art Kyoto (MoCA Kyoto):
This museum focuses on modern and contemporary art and is located in Okazaki Park. Its thought-provoking exhibitions frequently include renowned international artists as well as local talents. Insider knowledge: Check out their event calendar—they regularly host fascinating talks and art-related events.

Yamamoto Bijutsuten: Yamamoto Bijutsuten, a cozy gallery in the bustling district of Kawaramachi, is a treasure trove of traditional Japanese art. It's a feast for art lovers, with everything from woodblock prints to calligraphy on display. Insider tip: Spend some time talking with the staff; they're enthusiastic about the pieces and have fascinating stories to tell.

Kyoto Seika University Art Space: This university's gallery showcases emerging talents and student artworks. It's a hub for fresh perspectives and creative experimentation. Insider advice: Don't hesitate to interact with the artists—their enthusiasm is contagious!

Gallery Kura: Gallery Kura, located in Pontocho's atmospheric area, is dedicated to showcasing local crafts and traditional art forms. Visitors can see exquisite ceramics, textiles, and lacquerware. Insider tip: They frequently hold live demonstrations—don't pass up the opportunity to see artisans at work!

These galleries provide a wide range of artistic experiences, from avant-garde expressions to time-honored traditional crafts. Each gallery invites visitors to immerse themselves in Kyoto's vibrant and ever-changing art scene, whether it's exploring contemporary trends or delving into the depths of Japanese artistry. Keep an eye on their schedules for talks, workshops, and events that will enrich your artistic experience!

HIDDEN GEMS: LESSER-KNOWN MUSEUMS AND GALLERIES

The Nomura Art Museum:
Tucked away in a quiet corner near Nijo Castle, this gem houses exquisite traditional art pieces, including scrolls, ceramics, and lacquerware. Its serene ambiance and curated collection make it a haven for art enthusiasts seeking a deeper appreciation of Kyoto's cultural legacy. Insider advice: The garden view from the tearoom is a tranquil spot for reflection.

Asahi Beer Oyamazaki Villa Museum of Art:
Aside from its connection to beer, Asahi Brewery's museum houses an impressive collection of European and Japanese art. This villa-turned-museum on the outskirts of town astonishes visitors with its diverse exhibits and stunning architecture. Insider tip: The villa's garden provides a

tranquil haven for contemplation after exploring the exhibits.

Kyoto International Woodblock Print Symposium Museum:
A true hidden treasure for fans of woodblock prints! This small museum, tucked away in a peaceful neighborhood, displays a variety of prints and hosts symposiums to delve into the intricate art of woodblock printing. Insider tip: Talk to the staff; they'll tell you fascinating stories about the prints and techniques.

Kyoto University Museum:
This museum, nestled on the campus of Kyoto University, is frequently overlooked by visitors. It houses a diverse collection, including archaeological artifacts and natural history specimens. It's a lesser-known treasure trove that reveals Kyoto's scientific and historical legacies. Insider tip: Keep an eye out for their special exhibitions, which frequently explore unusual topics.

The Tofukuji Temple Museum:
This museum, located next to the iconic Tofukuji Temple, is a hidden gem. It hosts seasonal exhibitions that complement the temple's tranquil atmosphere. Visitors can enjoy the tranquility of the temple grounds while exploring a diverse array of artifacts and artworks. Insider tip: Combine a visit

to the temple with a visit to the museum for a more complete experience.

The Museum of Furuta Oribe and Ceramics:
This museum honors the legacy of Furuta Oribe, a renowned tea master and ceramist, and is located in Gojozaka's pottery district. Its intimate setting highlights Oribe ware while also providing a deeper understanding of Japanese tea culture. Join one of their tea ceremonies for an immersive experience in traditional rituals.

Kyoto's lesser-known museums and galleries provide intimate encounters with the city's cultural tapestry. They may not always appear at the top of guidebooks, but they do reveal hidden gems for those looking for unique and off-the-beaten-path experiences. Don't rush through their stories—immerse yourself in them to discover the soul of Kyoto's lesser-explored artistic and historical narratives!

CHAPTER 8

KYOTO'S FOOD AND DRINK

OVERVIEW OF KYOTO'S FOOD AND DRINK SCENE

Kyoto's culinary landscape is a tantalizing tapestry woven with centuries of tradition and innovation. Renowned as a haven for authentic Japanese cuisine, the city offers a diverse culinary journey that transcends the ordinary.

Overview of Kyoto's Food and Drink Scene:

Kyoto's food scene is a celebration of tradition, craftsmanship, and the artistry of Japanese cuisine. From refined kaiseki multi-course meals to street-side yatai stalls, Kyoto presents an array of culinary experiences. The city's historical significance as the former imperial capital has influenced its gastronomy, preserving ancient recipes and culinary techniques passed down through generations.

The pinnacle of Kyoto's culinary art, Kaiseki cuisine, is an elaborate feast that meticulously showcases seasonal ingredients and embodies the spirit of omotenashi (hospitality). Meanwhile, the bustling Nishiki Market is a gastronomic paradise—a lively alley lined with stalls selling everything from pickled vegetables to freshly prepared seafood and sweets.

Kyoto is also well-known for its tea culture, where matcha reigns supreme. Visitors can partake in traditional tea ceremonies and matcha-flavored treats ranging from delicate wagashi sweets to matcha-infused noodles and ice cream.

Kyoto embraces innovation in addition to tradition. Classic dishes are reinterpreted and presented with a modern twist in modern cafes and restaurants. Hidden izakayas tucked away in narrow alleys offer a glimpse into local nightlife, serving regional sake and flavorful small plates.

The city's commitment to preserving culinary heritage extends to its use of seasonal ingredients. Each season brings with it a new menu that celebrates nature's bounty—cherry blossoms in spring, fresh vegetables in summer, the harvest in autumn, and the delicate flavors of winter.

Kyoto's food and drink scene entices both gourmands and curious foodies to embark on an enthralling journey. Kyoto is a treasure trove of culinary delights, inviting visitors to taste the essence of Japanese culture with every dish, whether it's savoring centuries-old recipes, indulging in street food, or exploring innovative dining experiences.

MUST-TRY DISHES IN KYOTO

Kyoto is a culinary treasure trove, and here are three must-try dishes along with some excellent spots to savor them:

Kaiseki Ryori

This multi-course haute cuisine is an artful expression of Kyoto's culinary mastery. It's a symphony of seasonal ingredients meticulously prepared to delight the senses. Try it at Gion Karyo, a Michelin-starred restaurant known for its exquisite kaiseki experience. For a more intimate setting, Hiiragiya, a traditional ryokan, offers a personalized kaiseki meal in a historic atmosphere.

Yudofu

Yudofu is a simple yet divine dish that consists of a hot pot of tofu simmered in a delicate kombu broth. It exemplifies

Kyoto's devotion to purity and simplicity. Visit Tousuiro in the tranquil Nanzenji area to enjoy this dish in a traditional setting. Alternatively, for a more modern take on this Kyoto classic, visit Yudofu Sagano.

Obanzai

These are Kyoto-style dishes made with local vegetables and ingredients. Menami is a great place to try obanzai in a cozy, welcoming setting. This Gion district restaurant serves a rotating menu of seasonal dishes prepared with meticulous attention to detail.

Kyo-kaiseki

Kyoto's local and seasonal ingredients are highlighted in this refined version of kaiseki cuisine. Experience it at Gion Nanba, a renowned restaurant that offers a modern twist on this traditional fare. Giro Giro Hitoshina offers innovative twists on kyo-kaiseki in an artsy setting for a more intimate setting.

Sushi

While not originally from Kyoto, the city boasts exceptional sushi. At Sushi Gion Matsudaya, indulge in top-quality sushi crafted by skilled chefs in an intimate setting. Alternatively, Kappa Sushi near the Nishiki Market offers a casual dining experience with fresh and reasonably priced sushi.

Kitsune Udon

This Kyoto favorite udon dish features sweet fried tofu atop noodles in a savory broth. Mimikou, a cozy restaurant near Nijo Castle known for its flavorful kitsune udon, is a great place to try it. Another recommended restaurant is Omen, which serves handmade udon noodles in a tranquil garden setting.

Yuba

Yuba is a delicate and nutritious ingredient made from the skin of soybean milk. Shoraian, nestled in the Arashiyama bamboo grove, serves yuba-centric cuisine in beautiful natural surroundings. Kanei, located near the famous Kinkaku-ji Temple, also serves yuba-based dishes in a traditional setting.

Each of these dishes exemplifies Kyoto's culinary heritage, demonstrating the city's commitment to quality, tradition, and seasonality. Whether in a fine dining establishment or a casual eatery, these dishes invite you to savor Kyoto's flavors in a variety of authentic settings.

BEST RESTAURANTS IN KYOTO

Kikunoi Honten (Gion Kikunoi)

Nestled in the historic Gion district, Kikunoi Honten is a three-Michelin-starred restaurant famed for its exquisite kaiseki meals. The chef, Yoshihiro Murata, masterfully crafts seasonal dishes that celebrate Kyoto's flavors. Book a counter seat for an intimate dining experience, and if you're lucky, Chef Murata might even personally attend to your table. Insider tip: Opt for a lunch reservation for a more affordable yet equally delightful kaiseki experience.

Izuju

This traditional Kyoto-style sushi restaurant in Gion has been serving delectable pressed sushi (known as oshizushi) for over a century. The sabazushi, featuring mackerel, is a local favorite. Insider advice: The restaurant tends to get busy, so aim to visit during off-peak hours for a more relaxed dining experience.

Ganko Sushi

Ganko Sushi, which has several locations throughout Kyoto, combines tradition and innovation in its sushi offerings. Their beautifully presented sushi platters feature the freshest seafood available. Visit their Pontocho location for riverside dining with picturesque views. Insider tip: Don't miss their seasonal offerings, which frequently feature Kyoto delicacies.

Okutan Kiyomizu

This restaurant, located near Kiyomizu-dera Temple, specializes in yudofu—soft tofu simmered in a flavorful broth. The ambiance, set in a historic wooden building, complements the simple yet exquisite flavors of the yudofu.

Reservations are strongly advised, especially during peak tourist seasons, to ensure a table with a view of the temple.

Yoshikawa:

This Michelin-starred establishment in the Gion district is renowned for its delicate tempura. Prepared by skilled chefs, the tempura dishes feature fresh ingredients, each fried to perfection. Insider tip: Go for the counter seats to witness the artistry of tempura preparation up close.

Hyotei

Hyotei is a long-standing culinary institution known for its traditional kaiseki meals served in a tranquil tea-house setting. This Michelin-starred restaurant in Higashiyama has been delighting guests for over 400 years. Insider tip: Reserve a private room to enjoy your meal in peace and quiet.

Gion Kappa

This unassuming Gion eatery serves authentic Kyoto-style shabu-shabu, a hot pot dish with thinly sliced meat and vegetables cooked in a flavorful broth. The warm ambiance and attentive service enhance the dining experience. Insider tip: Ask the staff for advice on the best cuts of meat and dipping sauces.

Ippodo Tea Co.

For a quintessential Kyoto tea experience, visit Ippodo Tea Co. near the Nishiki Market. This centuries-old tea shop offers an extensive selection of high-quality matcha and green teas. Sit at the tea room and savor their matcha-based beverages and traditional sweets. Insider tip: Join one of their tea workshops for an immersive understanding of Japanese tea culture.

Gogyo Ramen

Gogyo Ramen's signature Kogashi Miso Ramen features charred miso broth that adds a smoky depth to the dish and is known for its innovative take on ramen. The modern ambiance and flavorful ramen bowls make it a popular choice for both locals and visitors. Insider tip: Get there early to avoid long lines during peak hours.

Chao Chao Gyoza

This gyoza restaurant in downtown Kyoto is a must-see for gyoza fans. Their gyoza, which has a crispy exterior and juicy fillings, is available in a variety of flavors, including traditional pork and unique vegetarian options. Insider tip: For an extra burst of flavor, pair your gyoza with one of their homemade dipping sauces.

Each of these Kyoto restaurants offers a distinct culinary experience, whether it's savoring meticulously crafted kaiseki, enjoying traditional sushi, sampling Kyoto's regional specialties, or learning the art of tempura. Booking ahead of time, going during off-peak hours, and choosing counter seats can all improve the dining experience, allowing visitors to fully immerse themselves in Kyoto's culinary delights.

BEST BARS AND CAFES IN KYOTO

Bars:

Bar K6: Tucked away in Pontocho, this intimate jazz bar exudes old-world charm and offers an extensive selection of whiskies and cocktails. Insider tip: Arrive early to snag a seat at the counter and enjoy live jazz performances in a cozy setting.

The Common One Kyoto: A hip rooftop bar in the city center with panoramic views of Kyoto Tower and the city skyline. Enjoy craft cocktails, local beers, and a lively atmosphere. Insider tip: The sunset hours are magical here—arrive early to secure a vantage point.

Beer Komachi: Located near Kiyomizu-dera, this craft beer bar features an array of local and international brews. The cozy atmosphere and friendly staff make it a great spot to sample unique beers. Insider advice: Don't hesitate to ask the staff for recommendations; they're passionate about their craft.

Bungalow: A chic cocktail bar in Gion known for its creative cocktails and stylish ambiance. The bartenders here are passionate about mixology and meticulously craft each drink. Insider tip: Order one of their signature concoctions and strike up a conversation with the friendly staff to get personalized drink recommendations.

Mujyaki: A whiskey bar hidden near Yasaka Shrine that offers an extensive selection of rare Japanese whiskies. For whiskey enthusiasts, the intimate setting and knowledgeable bartender create a welcoming environment. Insider tip: Request a whiskey flight to sample a variety of premium labels.

Campbell Early: Tucked away in a historic building in downtown Kyoto, this sophisticated cocktail bar with a speakeasy vibe. The ambiance is classic elegance, and the skilled bartenders create exquisite drinks tailored to your tastes. Due to limited seating, reservations are strongly advised.

Cafes:

% Arabica: Known for its minimalist design and exceptional coffee, this cafe has become an iconic spot for coffee enthusiasts. Try their single-origin brews while enjoying the riverside view at the Arashiyama branch. Insider tip: The early morning hours offer a tranquil setting before the crowds arrive.

Walden Woods Kyoto: This charming cafe, tucked away in a quiet neighborhood, provides a tranquil respite from the bustling city. While relaxing in the cozy ambiance, savor their delicious pastries and aromatic coffee. Insider tip: For a more secluded atmosphere, check out their second-floor seating.

Cafe Bibliotic Hello!: A book lover's paradise, this cafe in Shimogyo offers a cozy space filled with books where you can enjoy coffee and light bites. The serene ambiance and the chance to browse through various genres make it a perfect spot for relaxation. Insider advice: Visit during weekdays for a quieter experience.

Weekenders Coffee: This hip cafe near Nijo Castle specializes in specialty coffee and has a relaxed atmosphere. While soaking in the local atmosphere, enjoy their expertly brewed coffee and delectable pastries. Insider tip: Try to get a seat near the window to people-watch.

Kurasu Kyoto: A coffee lover's paradise featuring specialty coffee from around the world. The minimalist decor and expertly brewed coffee make it a coffee lover's paradise.

Insider tip: Try their pour-over coffee and chat with the baristas—they're enthusiastic about their work.

Inoda Coffee Honten: A venerable 1947 establishment known for its classic coffeehouse ambiance and meticulously brewed coffee. Step into the retro atmosphere and sip their signature blend with a slice of their famous coffee jelly. Insider tip: It can get crowded, so go early in the morning.

Kissako Uji Main Store: This traditional tea house in Uji, known for its matcha, provides a tranquil setting in which to enjoy matcha-based drinks and traditional sweets. Sit on the tatami mats and enjoy the tranquillity while indulging in authentic matcha delicacies. Insider tip: For a delectable treat, try their matcha parfait.

Kyoto's bars and cafes provide a variety of experiences, ranging from hidden jazz bars to trendy rooftop lounges and quaint book-filled cafes. Consider exploring during off-peak hours for a more relaxed atmosphere and engaging with locals and staff for personalized recommendations and insights into Kyoto's vibrant nightlife and cafe culture to make the most of your visit.

CHAPTER 9

KYOTO'S SHOPPING SCENE

OVERVIEW OF KYOTO'S SHOPPING SCENE

Kyoto's shopping scene is a captivating blend of tradition and modernity, offering a diverse array of shopping experiences that cater to every taste and interest. From bustling markets to historic shopping streets and contemporary boutiques, every corner of Kyoto holds treasures waiting to be discovered.

Overview of Kyoto's Shopping Scene:

Historical Streets: Kyoto has charming streets such as Teramachi and Shinkyogoku, which are alive with traditional shops, vendors, and arcades. These bustling passageways are a veritable treasure trove of Japanese crafts, clothing, souvenirs, and regional delicacies. Visitors can experience the essence of Kyoto's rich cultural heritage by browsing through a plethora of shops selling kimono, pottery, tea, sweets, and intricate handicrafts.

Traditional Markets: The iconic Nishiki Market, known as "Kyoto's Kitchen," offers a sensory journey through narrow alleys filled with vendors selling fresh seafood, pickles, tea, and traditional snacks. The market's vibrant atmosphere immerses visitors in the local culinary and cultural delights.

Modern Shopping: Kyoto embraces modernity with modern shopping districts, in addition to its historical charm. Porta and Isetan in Kyoto Station offer a fusion of international and Japanese brands, fashion boutiques, and department stores catering to a wide range of tastes. Visitors can visit modern shopping malls such as Kyoto BAL, which offer a mix of local and global brands.

Specialty Stores: Kyoto is well-known for its specialty shops specializing in traditional crafts and arts. From renowned pottery shops in the Kiyomizu pottery district to exquisite tea houses in Uji, these establishments preserve age-old techniques and provide discerning shoppers with unique, artisanal products.

Kyoto's shopping scene caters to a wide range of preferences, whether you're looking for traditional crafts, local delicacies, stylish fashion, or modern amenities. Each shopping district has its own distinct personality, providing an immersive experience that reflects the city's rich cultural heritage as well as its embrace of modern trends. The diverse shopping landscape of Kyoto reveals a tapestry of offerings, making it a haven for shoppers seeking both tradition and modernity in their retail experiences.

BEST SHOPPING DISTRICTS IN KYOTO

Kyoto's shopping districts offer unique experiences, each with its own charm and specialty. Here's a rundown of some of the best shopping districts in Kyoto along with insider advice:

Teramachi and Shinkyogoku Shopping Arcade: In downtown Kyoto, these adjoining covered arcades form a bustling shopping district brimming with traditional and modern shops. Teramachi's tranquillity and Shinkyogoku's vibrancy appeal to a wide range of tastes. Insider insight: For great deals on kimono, accessories, souvenirs, and local snacks, look for tax-free stores and seasonal sales.

Nishiki Market: Known as the "Kitchen of Kyoto," this historic market is a food lover's paradise. Stroll through narrow alleys filled with vendors offering fresh seafood, pickles, sweets, and traditional Kyoto delicacies. Insider advice: Haggle politely for discounts, and explore the market during off-peak hours for a more relaxed shopping experience.

Gion District: Gion, known for its historic charm and tea houses, offers a refined shopping experience. Hanami-koji Street's boutique shops sell high-quality souvenirs, traditional crafts, and elegant kimonos. Insider tip: Explore the side streets for smaller shops that often offer unique items at lower prices than the main thoroughfares.

Kyoto Station and Porta: Kyoto Station, a hub for travelers, houses a variety of shopping areas. Porta, an underground shopping mall, houses a variety of fashion boutiques, souvenir shops, and restaurants. Insider tip: Take advantage of tourist information centers to obtain discount coupons and tax-free shopping opportunities.

Kawaramachi and Pontocho: These adjacent Kamo River districts are teeming with trendy boutiques, department stores, and specialty shops. The retail outlets in Kawaramachi cater to the latest fashion trends, whereas the riverside charm of Pontocho offers a mix of traditional and modern establishments. Insider tip: Look for hidden gems and local artisans on side streets, and consider visiting during festivals for special discounts and events.

Kyoto Handicraft Center: Located near Heian Shrine, this center showcases a wide array of traditional crafts from Kyoto and beyond. Visitors can find pottery, textiles, lacquerware, and other handmade items. Insider tip: Look for demonstration events to witness craftsmen at work and learn about their artistry.

Arashiyama: Arashiyama, famous for its bamboo grove and scenic beauty, also offers charming shopping experiences. The area surrounding Tenryu-ji Temple has shops selling traditional crafts, sweets, and one-of-a-kind souvenirs. Insider tip: Go beyond the main street to find quieter shops and local artisans selling handmade goods.

Fushimi: Besides being known for its stunning torii gates at Fushimi Inari Taisha, the area has local shops offering sake-related products. Sake breweries and shops sell an array of sake varieties and related items, making it a great spot for sake enthusiasts. Insider's tip: Some breweries offer free tastings, so inquire about tasting sessions.

Kyoto Handicraft Center in Gion: This center in the heart of Gion displays a wide range of traditional crafts, such as pottery, textiles, fans, and decorative items. Insider tip: Use the center's workshops to create your crafts and gain a deeper understanding of traditional craftsmanship.

Daimaru Kyoto: Situated near Shijo-Karasuma, Daimaru is a renowned department store offering a wide range of goods, from high-end fashion to local souvenirs. The store has tax-free counters and seasonal sales, making it a one-stop shopping destination. Insider's insight: Check for special events or promotions to score discounts on luxury brands.

Kyoto Antique Markets: Periodic antique markets, such as Toji Temple's Kobo-san Market and Kitano Tenmangu Shrine's Tenjin-san Market, provide a delightful treasure hunt. Vintage items, antiques, kimono, and unique collectibles are available to visitors. Insider tip: Bargaining is common, so practice your negotiating skills if you want to get a good deal.

Exploring these districts allows visitors to delve deeper into Kyoto's varied shopping scene, whether they are looking for traditional crafts, unique souvenirs, or modern retail therapy. Embracing the local culture and taking advantage of special events, seasonal sales, and occasional free tastings can enhance the shopping experience in Kyoto.

MUST-VISIT MARKETS IN KYOTO

Kyoto boasts several vibrant markets, each offering a unique experience and a glimpse into the city's culture. Here are some must-visit markets in Kyoto along with reasons why they're essential stops for visitors:

Nishiki Market

Known as "Kyoto's Kitchen," Nishiki Market is an iconic culinary destination offering a dazzling array of fresh produce, seafood, local snacks, and traditional ingredients. Visitors can immerse themselves in Kyoto's culinary heritage by exploring the narrow alleys lined with vendors. Don't leave without trying the freshly prepared skewered snacks or sampling local delicacies like pickles, sweets, and fresh sashimi. The market's vibrant atmosphere and diverse offerings make it an essential stop for food enthusiasts and anyone curious about Kyoto's gastronomic delights.

Tenjin-san Market at Kitano Tenmangu Shrine:
This traditional flea market, held on the 25th of every month, embodies the spirit of Kyoto's history and culture. Stroll through the antiques, kimono, pottery, vintage items, and handicrafts stalls. Visitors can find one-of-a-kind treasures while relaxing in the serene atmosphere of the shrine. Don't miss out on exploring the local arts and crafts, interacting with vendors, and possibly finding a one-of-a-kind souvenir to take home. The market's

combination of history, local artistry, and vibrant energy provides an enriching cultural experience.

Toji Temple Kobo-san Market
This market, held on the 21st of each month at Toji Temple, is one of Kyoto's largest and oldest flea markets. It's a treasure trove for antique lovers and collectors, with items ranging from pottery and ceramics to vintage kimono, Buddhist items, and handicrafts. The lively market atmosphere, combined with the opportunity to find one-of-a-kind and authentic Japanese artifacts, makes it an unmissable destination for those seeking cultural immersion and unique souvenirs.

Kyoto Handicraft Center Market
This market, located within the Kyoto Handicraft Center in Gion, features a wide range of traditional crafts, handmade items, and artisanal products. Visitors can peruse stalls selling pottery, textiles, lacquerware, and other fine crafts. Interacting with skilled artisans, watching live demonstrations, and purchasing genuine handmade souvenirs directly from the creators make this market a cultural immersion as well as a valuable shopping experience.

Kyoto flea markets in temples and shrines (Various Locations):

Several temples and shrines in Kyoto host flea markets throughout the year, offering a diverse range of goods such as antiques, vintage kimono, tea utensils, artworks, and more. These markets frequently offer a tranquil setting within temple or shrine grounds, allowing visitors to combine spiritual exploration with treasure hunting. Each market has a distinct selection of items, making them worthwhile for those looking for authentic and unique finds while learning about the cultural significance of the temples and shrines.

Visiting these markets allows travelers to engage with Kyoto's vibrant culture, interact with locals, and discover the city's culinary and artisanal heritage. The markets' diverse offerings, authentic experiences, and the opportunity to find unique, locally made treasures are compelling reasons why no visit to Kyoto is complete without exploring these bustling and culturally rich hubs.

BEST SOUVENIRS TO BUY IN KYOTO

Kyoto offers an array of unique and culturally rich souvenirs that encapsulate the essence of the city's heritage. Here are some of the best souvenirs to consider bringing back from Kyoto:

1. Traditional Japanese Crafts: Kyoto is renowned for its traditional crafts, including pottery (such as Kiyomizu-yaki and Kyo-yaki), exquisite textiles (like Nishijin-ori silk fabrics and yuzen-dyed items), lacquerware, and fans. These meticulously crafted items showcase centuries-old techniques and make for elegant and timeless souvenirs.

2. Kyoto Tea: Kyoto is well-known for its tea culture, and it has a wide selection of high-quality teas, particularly matcha (powdered green tea) and sencha (steeped green tea). For an authentic taste of Kyoto's tea tradition, look for tea packs from reputable tea houses or souvenir shops.

3. Yatsuhashi: Yatsuhashi, a popular Kyoto confection, is a type of sweet made from glutinous rice flour that is typically filled with red bean paste and flavored with cinnamon. These delicate treats are available in a variety of flavors and packaging, making them ideal edible souvenirs.

4. Furoshiki: These versatile and beautifully designed cloth wraps are used for various purposes, such as gift wrapping, carrying items, or as decorative accents. Furoshiki come in a variety of patterns and sizes, showcasing traditional Japanese aesthetics.

5. Japanese Fans (Sensu): Kyoto is well-known for its sensu, or folding fans. These elegant fans are available in a variety of designs, ranging from traditional motifs to modern styles, and can be found in souvenir shops and craft stores throughout the city.

6. *Wagashi:* Delicate and intricately crafted Japanese sweets, known as wagashi, are a delightful and edible souvenir. These seasonal and artistic treats, often made from ingredients like sweet bean paste and mochi, are available in Kyoto's confectionery shops.

7. *Chopsticks (Hashi):* Look for beautifully crafted chopsticks made of materials like wood, lacquer, or bamboo. Some stores also sell personalized and handcrafted chopsticks, which make for a useful and thoughtful souvenir.

Kyoto's rich cultural heritage, craftsmanship, and traditions are embodied in each of these souvenirs. Consider the authenticity, quality, and story they tell about Kyoto's history and artisanal excellence when purchasing souvenirs. These souvenirs not only make great gifts, but they also serve as tangible reminders of the unique experiences and cultural immersion that can be found in Kyoto.

CHAPTER 10

KYOTO'S FESTIVALS AND EVENTS

MUST-SEE FESTIVALS IN KYOTO

Kyoto hosts vibrant festivals throughout the year, each offering a glimpse into the city's rich cultural heritage and traditions. Here are some must-see festivals in Kyoto with insider tips:

Gion Matsuri (Gion Festival): One of Japan's most famous festivals, Gion Matsuri takes place throughout July. The grand procession, known as the Yamahoko Junko, features elaborately decorated floats parading through the streets of central Kyoto. Insider tip: Arrive early to secure a good viewing spot along the parade route, especially near Shijo Street and Kawaramachi.

Aoi Matsuri (Hollyhock Festival): Held on May 15th, this ancient festival features a procession from the Kyoto Imperial Palace to Shimogamo Shrine and Kamigamo Shrine. Participants don traditional Heian-era attire, including court nobles, priests, and warriors, creating a striking visual spectacle. Insider's insight: Catch a glimpse of the procession as it passes through the Kyoto streets or watch the main event at Shimogamo Shrine.

Jidai Matsuri (Festival of Ages): This festival, held on October 22nd, celebrates Kyoto's history. Participants in period costumes march from the Imperial Palace to the Heian Shrine. The procession depicts historical figures and events from various eras. Insider tip: For the best views of the parade, stand near the Imperial Palace or the Heian Shrine along the route.

Daimonji Gozan Okuribi (Daimonji Fire Festival): This
event, which takes place on August 16th, marks the end of
the O-Bon season. On five mountaintops around Kyoto,
massive bonfires are lit, creating iconic characters and
symbols. Insider tip: For a panoramic view of the illuminated
characters, head to high vantage points such as
Daimonji-yama or Funaoka-yama.

***Hanatoro (Arashiyama Kimono Forest and Bamboo
Light-Up):*** A winter illumination event held in Arashiyama
typically in December. The serene beauty of Arashiyama's
bamboo grove is enhanced by thousands of lanterns lining
the paths. Insider's insight: Visit during the evening to
witness the bamboo forest transformed into a magical,
ethereal space.

Kurama no Hi Matsuri (Kurama Fire Festival): Taking
place on October 22nd, this dramatic festival held in Kurama

involves a procession of locals carrying massive torches. The procession culminates in a fiery spectacle on Mount Kurama. Insider's tip: Arrive early to secure a good viewing spot and witness the mesmerizing torch-lit procession.

Miyako Odori (Cherry Blossom Dance): Miyako Odori is a series of traditional dance performances by geisha and maiko held in the Gion district in April. Elegant dances, music, and kimono fashion are featured in the captivating performances. Insider tip: Purchase tickets in advance to ensure a seat and enjoy this iconic Kyoto cultural experience.

Visitors can immerse themselves in Kyoto's cultural heritage and witness the city's vibrant traditions by attending these festivals. Consider arriving early, familiarizing yourself with the festival routes, and respecting local customs and traditions while enjoying the lively atmosphere and stunning displays to fully appreciate these events.

MUST-SEE EVENTS IN KYOTO

In addition to festivals, Kyoto hosts various captivating events throughout the year that showcase its cultural richness. Here are some must-see events in Kyoto along with insider insights:

Kyoto Arashiyama Hanatouro: This event typically takes place in December. The Arashiyama district, known for its stunning bamboo grove, is illuminated with thousands of lanterns. Visitors can stroll along the illuminated paths and experience the ethereal beauty of Arashiyama at night. Insider tip: Visit the area during weekdays or earlier hours to avoid crowds.

Kyoto International Manga Anime Fair: This annual event in September celebrates Japanese pop culture with manga, anime, cosplay, exhibitions, and stage performances. It's a fantastic opportunity to immerse yourself in the world of manga and anime while enjoying interactive exhibits and exclusive merchandise. Check out the schedule for panel discussions and special guest appearances.

Kyoto Imperial Palace Open House: This event, held twice a year in spring and autumn, allows visitors to visit normally restricted areas of the Imperial Palace. Guided tours allow visitors to explore the palace grounds, admire the architecture, and learn about Kyoto's imperial history. Insider tip: Arrive early because space is limited, and consider joining one of the guided tours to gain a better understanding of the palace's significance.

Kyoto Takigi Noh at Heian Shrine: This traditional Noh theater performance illuminated by torchlight takes place in autumn. The ancient art form of Noh is performed against the backdrop of the Heian Shrine gardens, creating a mystical ambiance. Insider's tip: Secure tickets in advance and arrive early to enjoy the serene atmosphere and cultural spectacle.

Kyoto Higashiyama Hanatoro: This event, which takes place in the spring and winter, illuminates the Higashiyama district with lanterns, creating a magical nighttime atmosphere along the historic streets. Visitors can take in the traditional atmosphere as well as the captivating views of illuminated temples and shrines. Wear comfortable shoes when walking and exploring the scenic pathways.

Attending these events allows visitors to delve deeper into Kyoto's cultural tapestry and provides unique opportunities to witness traditional arts, immerse in local customs, and experience the vibrant atmosphere of the city. Participating in these events broadens one's understanding of Kyoto's history and provides memorable glimpses of the city's timeless charm.

HIDDEN GEMS: LESSER-KNOWN FESTIVALS AND EVENTS

While Kyoto is known for its prominent festivals and events, there are hidden gems—lesser-known festivals and events—that offer unique experiences. Here are a few of them:

Kifune-jinja Water Festival: Held at Kifune Shrine in July, this event celebrates the deity of water. Participants pray for safety during the rainy season and receive special paper amulets. A highlight is the Nagoshi-no-harae ritual, where people walk through a ring made of sedge grass. Insider tip: Combine your visit with exploring the serene Kibune area and dining at the riverside restaurants offering kawadoko (patio dining over the river).

Kyoto Sake Matsuri (Sake Festival): This event, held in March, highlights Kyoto's sake breweries. It is held at various locations and allows visitors to sample a variety of local sake varieties, learn about the brewing process, and interact with brewers. Insider tip: Buy a sake-tasting ticket in advance to avoid long lines and sample a wide range of Kyoto's finest brews.

Kyoto Nippon Festival: This autumn festival honors traditional Japanese performing arts such as Noh, Kyogen, and other classical art forms. It's a cultural extravaganza with performances by renowned artists that will give you a better understanding of Japan's theatrical heritage. Insider tip: Check the schedule ahead of time and purchase tickets for specific performances to see the artistry up close.

Kurama Hi Matsuri (Kurama Fire Festival, Fire Walk): On October 22nd, Kurama village hosts this dramatic event where participants walk on hot coals to pray for protection and good health. The ceremony is held at Kurama Temple, and the spiritual fervor during the fire-walking ritual is an awe-inspiring sight. Insider's tip: Arrive early and explore the scenic Kurama area before the event begins.

Tango no Sekku (Boy's Day): This festival, held on May 5th at Shimogamo Shrine, is dedicated to the healthy development of boys. Families bring samurai helmet displays and bright koinobori (carp-shaped windsocks) to pray for the well-being of their sons. Insider tip: Attend this family-friendly celebration to witness this local tradition and explore the serene grounds of the shrine.

These Kyoto hidden gem festivals and events provide unique cultural insights, opportunities to engage with local traditions, and highlight the city's lesser-known yet captivating celebrations. Attending these events allows visitors to learn about authentic cultural practices as well as lesser-known aspects of Kyoto's vibrant heritage.

CHAPTER 11

KYOTO'S SURROUNDING AREAS

DAY TRIPS FROM KYOTO

Explore Dynamic Osaka

Travel time: Approximately 30 minutes

Osaka, a bustling metropolis with modern amenities, historical landmarks, and delicious food, is just a brief train ride from Kyoto. This urban playground is a great option for a day trip, blending traditional and modern elements.

Begin your day with a trip to Dotonbori, the iconic entertainment district of Osaka. Experience the colorful neon lights, stroll through the lively shopping areas, and indulge in street food dishes like takoyaki (spicy car) and okonomiyaki (riced pancakes). It's a great opportunity to take a photo with the iconic Glico Running Man billboard.

A cultural enclave, Osaka Castle is a representation of the city's history. Take a stroll through the grand castle grounds, discover its historical importance during Japan's feudal era, and admire panoramic views from the topmost floor.

When time permits, head to Shinsekai, a nostalgic spot known for its antiquated architecture and delectable kushikatsu (deep-fried wings). Trek around Tsutenkaku Tower to have a bird's-eye view and experience the nostalgic feeling.

Take a rapid train from Kyoto Station to Osaka Station to reach Osaka. With a journey time of roughly 30 minutes, this destination is an exciting and easily accessible day trip from Kyoto.

Osaka offers an exciting day trip, full of activity, food, and festivities, offering visitors a glimpse into the heart of modern Japan's cultural life.

Discover Tranquil Uji

Travel time: Approximately 20-30 minutes

Experience the serenity of a day trip from Kyoto to Uji, an ancient and picturesque town famous for its green tea. Just a brief train journey from Kyoto Station will take you to this peaceful haven nestled along the Uji River.

Begin your excursion at the Byodo-in Temple, a UNESCO World Heritage Site recognized for its Phoenix Hall. Admire the graceful structures symbolizing Buddhist beliefs and stroll through the temple's tranquil gardens, capturing a sense of timeless elegance.

Explore Uji's tea culture by visiting either one of the local traditional tea houses or a nearby tea shop. Discover the delights of matcha-infused sweet treats like matcha soft serve or traditional tea ceremonies offered in charming teahouses. Don't miss out on the chance to visit Taiho-an, a tea house with a historical feel and a scenic view of the Uji River.

Enjoy the beauty of Uji River by strolling along its banks, perhaps even feasting on some ducks that call it home. The picturesque bridges and stunning scenery of Uji's riverfront are a perfect spot for a peaceful stroll.

Uji can be reached from Kyoto Station by taking a local train to JR Uji Station. The journey to Uji can be completed in around 20-30 minutes, making it a convenient day trip option from Kyoto.

Amidst a peaceful setting, rich cultural heritage, and tea-focused attractions, Uji is an ideal getaway from the hustle and bustle of the city, where visitors can immerse themselves in a world of peace and green tea delights.

Escape to Serene Ohara

Travel time: Approximately 1 hour

To unwind and escape Kyoto's bustling city life, take a day to explore Ohara, a tranquil mountain village situated on the northern edge of the city. With its picturesque scenery, ancient temples and rural charm, Ohara is a peaceful retreat located only an hour's drive from Kyoto.

Start your day with Sanzen-in Temple, a stunning Buddhist temple known for its peaceful atmosphere and impressive moss gardens. Enjoy the stillness as you wander through the temple grounds adorned with colorful foliage, serene ponds, and ancient sculptures.

Observe the picturesque streets of Ohara and discover charming local stores that sell pottery, crafts, and fresh produce. Don't forget to indulge in dishes such as yuba (tofu skin), which is a regional specialty with a delicate and unique flavor.

Explore the surrounding countryside and explore hidden treasures such as Hosen-in Temple, which boasts an ancient pine tree and a peaceful moss garden. Enjoy the tranquil surroundings and serene atmosphere of rural Japan.

By taking a bus from Kyoto Station to Ohara, you can reach Ohara. It takes approximately 1 hour to reach this village, offering a convenient and picturesque way to explore the area.

A day trip to Ohara, boasting its tranquil temples, serene surroundings and bucolic ambiance, offers travelers the chance to enjoy nature's delights and immerse themselves in the rural charm of rural Kyoto.

Discover Ancient Nara

Travel time: Approximately 1 hour

Experience a diverse range of cultures and traditions by taking a one-day excursion from Kyoto to Nara, Japan's ancient capital, which is a treasure trove of history and spirituality. With its UNESCO-listed temples, tranquil parks, and curious deer, Nara is a train ride that takes just an hour.

Embark on your journey at the Todai-ji Temple, an iconic Buddhist dwelling where stands the enormous Great Buddha (Daibutsu). Discover this impressive statue and explore the temple grounds adorned with ancient memorabilia and sculptures.

Walk through Nara Park, a vast green area with numerous temples and the presence of friendly deer believed to be divine messengers. Local suppliers sell deer crackers to feed these friendly animals and capture unforgettable moments amidst the park's natural splendor.

Visit Kasuga Taisha Shrine, where you can admire the vermilion-colored buildings and rows of dangling lanterns. The shrine's serene forested paths are illuminated by a multitude of lanterns, creating an illusion.

For an authentic experience, explore the historic district of Nara in Naramachi. Traverse the narrow streets that are dotted with traditional merchant houses, craft shops and charming cafes to discover Nara's history.

To get to Kyoto, take the JR Nara Line from Kyoto Station towards Nara Station. With a journey of roughly 1 hour, this ancient city is easily accessible.

For a day trip, Naraku is a must-see city due to its cultural significance, historic sites, and natural beauty; it offers a glimpse into Japan's rich history and the harmonious coexistence of Japan and nature.

Experience Hiroshima's Peace Memorial Park and Beyond

Travel time: Approximately 2 hours

Take advantage of the opportunity to experience a day trip around Hiroshima, a city that is both haunting and inspiring due to its resilience. Although the journey by Shinkansen (bullet train) is about 2 hours, Hiroshima is a significant and historically rich destination.

Commence your day at the Hiroshima Peace Memorial Park, which is named after the victims of the atomic bombing in 1945. Visit the Memorial Museum of Peace to learn about this tragic event and what it has done, and to gain a deeper understanding of the importance of peace and reconciliation.

Afterward, explore the famous Atomic Bomb Dome (Genbaku Dome), a UNESCO World Heritage Site that has preserved the remains of the bomb's epicenter. The object's skeletal structure is a stark reminder of the destructive effects of nuclear warfare.

Afterward, after commemorating at the park with your loved ones, take a short ferry ride to Miyajima Island, recognized for its floating torii gate at Itsukushima Shrine. Admire the recognizable vermilion gate, which appears to float on water during high tides, and marvel at the sacred temples, picturesque streets, and peaceful forests of the island.

Opt for local specialties like grilled oysters and momiji manju (maple leaf-shaped cakes with red bean paste) from the street vendors on Miyajima Island.

From Kyoto Station, take the Shinkansen (bullet train) which runs from Kyoto to Hiroshima Station. Getting there is approximately 2 hours and it's an efficient way to reach Hiroshima comfortably.

While taking a day trip can be challenging, the poignant history of Hiroshima, the Peace Memorial Park's importance and breathtaking scenery of Miyajima Island make it an emotionally moving and culturally enriching experience.

Relax in Tranquil Kinosaki Onsen

Travel time: Approximately 2.5 to 3 hours

Enjoy a rejuvenating dip at Kinosaki Onsen, a charming seaside hot spring town located off the coast of the Sea of Japan. A journey that lasts around 2.5 to 3 hours by train takes you to Kinosaki Onsen, a serene retreat known for its soothing hot springs and peaceful surroundings.

Upon arrival, enjoy the peacefulness and traditional charm of the town. There are seven public hot spring bathhouses, or "soto-yu," in Kinosaki, each with its own unique style and mineral content. Walk around the city in a yukati (casual kimono) and put on geta (wooden sandals), while enjoying the mineral-rich waters of the bathhouses.

Take a leisurely walk along the streets lined with willows, passing by charming boutiques, cafenos, and ryokan (traditional inns). Enjoy Tajima beef, fresh seafood and tasty crab dishes while enjoying the local flavours.

Take advantage of the magnificent panoramic views and take a leisurely walk to Mount Daishi, where you can find the Onsen-ji Temple. The descent affords you with awe-inspiring views of the town and seaside.

A limited express train will take you from Kyoto Station to Kinosaki Onsen Station. The journey takes a short time, roughly 2.5 to 3, in terms of time, for a scenic drive through the countryside.

Featuring a serene environment, therapeutic hot springs, and a nostalgic feel, Kinosaki Onsen is the perfect choice for a day trip where visitors can immerse themselves in Japan's ancient onsen culture and enjoy peaceful surroundings.

BEST PLACES TO STAY OUTSIDE KYOTO

Here are some recommendations for excellent accommodations outside Kyoto:

1. Arashiyama (Kyoto Prefecture):

Arashiyama is a tranquil retreat from the hustle and bustle of Kyoto, and a stay here offers an opportunity to explore its western outskirts. Consider a classic ryokan (Japanese inn) or a modern guesthouse situated near the bamboo plantation. Enjoy the sounds of nature, stroll along the Katsura River and indulge in kaiseki dishes. Insider Tip: Stay in hotels with private onsen (hot springs) to relax among beautiful landscapes.

2. Nara (Nara Prefecture):

With its rich history and calm atmosphere, Nara offers a variety of lodging options. Take advantage of a stay in a shukubo (temple lodge) near Nara Park to experience the city's past. Experience the traditional Buddhist ceremonies, indulge in vegetarian shojin ryori dishes, and participate in morning prayers. Tips from insiders: Stay near Kasuga Taisha Shrine for peaceful walks and stunning scenery.

3. Kinosaki Onsen (Hyogo Prefecture):

Kinosaki Onsen offers ryokans that offer a serene hot spring retreat, including elegant tatami rooms and fine dining kaiseki. You can choose to stay in a ryokan with private onsens or opt for a local experience at one of the public bathhouses. Take a leisurely walk in the town's cool streets in a yukata and geta. Get an insider tip: Some ryokans provide shuttle transportation, making it convenient to travel between the seven public bathhouses.

4. *Miyajima Island (Hiroshima Prefecture):*

From ryokans with stunning ocean views to cozy guesthouses near Itsukushima Shrine, Miyajima Island has it all. Taste authentic fare, savor some fresh seafood delicacies, and take in the charming floating torii gate. To experience the island's calmness, spend a night after day-trippers depart and visit the shrine during low tide.

5. *Kurama and Kibune (Kyoto Prefecture):*

Located in the mountains, Kurama and Kibune are both serene retreats. Enjoy the beauty of nature in a ryokan or minshuku (Japanese-style guesthouse). Explore the forest, visit Kurama-dera Temple, and dine at riverside eateries in Kibune. It's worth it during the warmer months to choose accommodations with kawadoko dining platforms above the river for a unique dinner experience.

6. Uji (Kyoto Prefecture):

Uji, known for its tea culture and historical sites, has several lodging options near the Uji River. Consider whether you prefer a ryokan with tea-themed rooms or a modern hotel with a view of the river. Take a trip to tea houses, taste matcha, and visit Byodo-in Temple. Tips from an insider: Stay in close proximity to Ujigami Shrine for peace of mind and easy access to local attractions.

7. Himeji (Hyogo Prefecture):

With its majestic Himeji Castle, which is a well-known attraction, Himeji also offers accommodation in various traditional ryokans and modern hotels. Enjoy samurai history by staying near the castle for easy access. Discover the castle's pristine design and stroll through the Koko-en Garden. Don't forget to book a place near Otemae-dori for shopping and dining opportunities.

8. Kobe (Hyogo Prefecture):

The port city of Kobe has a wide variety of accommodations. Opt for a hotel featuring admiring harbor views, or opt for a stay in a ryokan in the historic Kitano area. Kobe's Chinatown, beef rations in Kobe, and the mesmerizing Nunobiki Herb Gardens are all worth visiting. It's recommended to choose Sannomiya for its excellent transportation connections and lively nightlife.

9. Mount Koya (Wakayama Prefecture):

To achieve spirituality, consider staying in a shukubo (temple lodging) on Mount Koya. Stay overnight in a monastery, participate in morning prayers, and indulge in delicious vegetarian meals made with Buddhist meat. Journey to Okunoi Cemetery and witness the peaceful atmosphere on top of the sacred mountain. For an immersive experience, it's wise to stay during the morning prayer service in a temple.

Each of these destinations has its own unique character and charm, whether it's steeped in history, renowned for its stunning natural beauty, or celebrated because of the culture that surrounds it, offering visitors a wide range of unforgettable experiences away from Kyoto's bustling tourist hub.

HIDDEN GEMS: LESSER-KNOWN DESTINATIONS NEAR KYOTO

1. Ohara:

Benefits: Ohara, located northeast of Kyoto, boasts tranquil landscapes and serene temples, including Sanzen-in and Jakko-in. Visitors can enjoy scenic countryside views, explore lesser-known temples, and experience a quieter side of Kyoto. Insider Tip: Don't miss the autumn foliage in November, offering stunning hues of red and gold across the countryside.

2. Kurama and Kibune:

Situated in the mountains to the north of Kyoto, Kurama and Kibune offer lush forests, hiking trails, and religious sites such as the Kurama-dera Temple. Enthusiast can enjoy onsen baths, nature walks, and the Kifune Shrine's mystical atmosphere. An Insider Tip: In the summer, visit one of the many kawadoko (riverside terraces) in Kibune to enjoy traditional dishes.

3. Miyama:

Intriguing: Miyama, renowned for its thatched-roof farmhouses and picturesque surroundings, provides a glimpse into the traditional rural Japan. Visitors can also take advantage of the Kayabuki no Sato preservation district, participate in cultural activities and enjoy the peaceful nature of the countryside. Get the insider tip by staying in a minshuku or farmhouse for an authentic rural experience.

4. *Amanohashidate:*

Amanohashidate, situated in the northern part of Kyoto Prefecture, is renowned for its magnificent sandbar, which is considered one of Japan's "Three Views." Guests can unwind on the beach, rent bicycles to explore the area, and take in the scenic views of Kasamatsu Park. A useful Insider Tip: Visit during sunrise or sunset to catch a breathtaking view of the sandbar from the viewpoint.

5. *Wazuka:*

Spotlight: The tea-growing region of Wazuka, south of Kyoto, is known for its picturesque terraced fields, tea plantations, and tea-related attractions. Guests can engage in tea picking, learn about tea cultivation, and take leisurely walks through the fields. Take advantage of a tea workshop or excursion to learn about tea production by visiting local farmers.

Each of these lesser-known spots near Kyoto offers travelers an opportunity to explore quieter and more authentic locales, enjoy the beauty of nature's bounty, or simply appreciate Japan's rich cultural heritage.

CHAPTER 12

IMPORTANT INFORMATION

MONEY SAVING TIPS WHILE AT KYOTO

1. Kyoto City Bus Pass:
Invest in a Kyoto City Bus Pass for unlimited rides on city buses. It offers convenience and cost savings, especially if you plan to explore multiple attractions in a day.

2. Kyoto Subway Pass:
If you intend to use the subway frequently, consider purchasing a Kyoto Subway Pass. It allows unlimited rides on the city's subway lines, saving you money on individual fares.

3. Bicycle Rentals:
Explore Kyoto on two wheels by renting a bicycle. Many shops offer affordable daily rentals, providing an economical and efficient way to visit various sights while enjoying the city's bike-friendly lanes.

4. Free Attractions and Activities:

Take advantage of free attractions like Kyoto's numerous temples and shrines with free entry. Stroll through historic districts like Gion or explore Nishiki Market without spending a penny.

5. Local Food Markets and Vendors:
Instead of dining at upscale restaurants, opt for local food markets or street vendors for affordable yet delicious meals. Nishiki Market is perfect for sampling Kyoto's culinary delights at reasonable prices.

6. Discounted Admission Tickets:
Consider combo tickets or discount passes for multiple attractions. Some passes offer reduced rates for popular sites, enabling savings if you plan to visit several places covered by the pass.

7. Early Bird Deals:
Take advantage of early morning specials at certain attractions or restaurants. Some temples and eateries offer discounted rates for visitors who arrive early.

8. Budget Accommodations:
Look beyond luxury hotels and consider budget-friendly accommodations such as guesthouses, hostels, or capsule hotels. Many provide comfortable stays at lower prices.

9. Water and Snacks:

Carry a refillable water bottle to stay hydrated and avoid purchasing bottled water frequently. Also, pack snacks or buy from local convenience stores to avoid overpriced snacks at tourist spots.

10. Off-Peak Travel:
If possible, plan your visit during off-peak seasons. Accommodation and transportation costs are often lower, and popular attractions are less crowded.

By incorporating these money-saving strategies, you can make the most of your visit to Kyoto without compromising your experiences while keeping your budget in check.

SUMMARY OF KYOTO AT A GLANCE

When Japan comes to mind, Tokyo and Kyoto often stand out. While Tokyo is the current capital, Kyoto held this prestigious position for an impressive span—from 794 to 1868—until governance transitioned from the Shogun to the Emperor.

Despite this historical change, Kyoto retains its allure as Japan's cultural nucleus. Boasting over a thousand temples and gardens, it's renowned as the nation's most picturesque city, steeped in cultural and historical significance.

Having explored numerous Japanese prefectures and cities, Kyoto remains exceptionally distinctive in my travels. Undoubtedly, it embodies the essence of traditional Japan, holding a special place as the heart and soul of the country's heritage.

GETTING AROUND KYOTO

Public Transportation:
Kyoto offers an extensive and convenient public transportation system, primarily comprising buses and a metro network. The city's buses, operated by multiple companies, form a comprehensive network that covers various attractions. Fares start at 230 JPY and are based on distance. Passengers must have exact change when disembarking and can acquire it from the machine near the driver. The metro system consists of two lines and over 30 stations, with fares ranging from 210 to 350 JPY.

Taxi:
Taxis are readily available in Kyoto, but they are more expensive, with starting fares of 600 JPY and additional kilometer charges. While they are convenient, due to the higher fares, travelers may prefer to use more cost-effective public transportation options.

Ride Sharing:

Didi and Uber are available in Kyoto for ridesharing services. However, the rates are often similar to taxi fares, making them less budget-friendly for transportation within the city compared to other options like buses or the metro.

Bicycle:

Exploring Kyoto by bicycle is a popular and inexpensive option. Standard bike rentals range from 800 to 1,000 JPY per day, while e-bike rentals range from 1,700 to 2,000 JPY. It's best to reserve a bike ahead of time or arrive early, especially during the summer months when demand is high. Visitors should be aware that traffic in Kyoto moves to the left.

Car Rental:

For those with an International Driving Permit (IDP), car rentals are an option, averaging around 7,500 JPY per day. However, driving in Kyoto follows the left side traffic pattern. Travelers must ensure they obtain the IDP before arriving in Japan and consider whether the convenience of a car justifies the higher expense compared to other transportation methods.

HOW TO STAY SAFE IN KYOTO.

Safety in Kyoto:

Kyoto, like Japan overall, is known for its high safety standards. Instances of robbery, scams, or violence are incredibly rare in the city.

Solo Travelers:

Solo female travelers should generally feel safe in Kyoto. While the city is secure, standard safety precautions remain essential, such as avoiding leaving drinks unattended in bars and refraining from walking alone when intoxicated. Occasionally, travelers might encounter incidents of lewd behavior, like inappropriate questions or catcalling. Women-only train cars during rush hours offer additional safety measures, marked by pink signs.

Scams and Security:

Scams are extremely rare in Kyoto, and visitors are unlikely to come across them. Maintain vigilance and awareness of your surroundings, however. Natural disasters such as earthquakes and typhoons are the most serious safety concerns in Japan. Be familiar with your hotel's emergency exits, download offline maps on your phone for emergency navigation, and keep Japan's emergency number (110) or the non-emergency Japan Helpline (0570-000-911) handy for assistance.

Travel Insurance:

Purchasing comprehensive travel insurance is highly recommended. It offers protection against illness, injury, theft, and trip cancellations. Having adequate travel insurance ensures coverage in case of any unforeseen circumstances, providing peace of mind during your travels.

WHEN TO VISIT KYOTO

Ideal Times to Visit Kyoto:
Summer, particularly June to August, marks the peak tourist season in Kyoto. However, it tends to be hot, with temperatures surpassing 32°C (89°F) and high humidity levels. Crowds are abundant, emphasizing the importance of early starts and pre-booking accommodations if you visit during this time.

Shoulder Seasons:
Kyoto is best visited between April and May, and between October and November. During these shoulder seasons, temperatures are cooler and rainfall is minimal. However, due to the cherry blossom season, late March to early April attracts crowds, so early bookings are advised for this popular time.

Winter in Kyoto:
Winter, while cold, is bearable, with daytime temperatures around 10°C (50°F) and nighttime temperatures around 1°C (34°F). During the winter, the city is noticeably quieter, and while snow is common, it usually melts quickly. Expect rain

and chilly weather, which will necessitate appropriate clothing.

Typhoon Season Precautions:
Kyoto, like much of Japan, experiences typhoon season from May to October. While Japan is well-prepared for typhoons, it's advisable to purchase travel insurance in advance for added security during this period of potential weather disturbances.

KYOTO TRAVEL RESTRICTIONS

Due to the ongoing global circumstances, the travel guidelines for Kyoto are constantly evolving. Booking.com offers a dedicated platform featuring comprehensive details on travel restrictions worldwide, including specific information on Kyoto.

Prior to organizing your journey to Kyoto, it's highly advisable to consult Booking.com for the most up-to-date travel restrictions in Japan. Additionally, if Kyoto is on your itinerary, it's wise to contemplate securing travel insurance that includes coverage for COVID-related incidents.

JAPAN VISA

Securing a visa for Japan can be a necessary step, depending on your passport and the purpose of your visit. To determine the specific requirements and whether a visa is needed for your trip to Japan, a helpful resource to explore is iVisa.com. This platform offers comprehensive information on visa requirements and facilitates the application process if a visa is indeed required for your travel plans.

WHERE TO EXCHANGE CURRENCY

In Japan, acquiring Japanese Yen (JPY) involves several options:

BANKS / POST OFFICES: While reliable, exchanging currency at Japanese banks or post offices can take time due to paperwork. The process usually takes around 30 minutes.

KINKEN SHOPS: Kinken shops, which are commonly found near major metro stations in major cities, exchange currency as well as sell event tickets. These stores' prices can be reasonable. For currency exchange in Kyoto, the Tokai Discount Ticket Shop is recommended.

CURRENCY EXCHANGE MACHINES: Although not widely available, currency exchange machines similar to ATMs can be found in certain locations. Insert foreign currency and receive the equivalent JPY swiftly. While less common in Kyoto, tourist and shopping areas might host them.

ATM MACHINES: ATMs in Japan, particularly those in convenience stores and post offices, are popular because they offer competitive rates. To avoid card blocking, make sure your bank is aware of your international transactions.

TIP: When prompted at an ATM for currency conversion, choose "WITHOUT conversion" to avoid unfavorable rates. Opting for conversion often results in the foreign bank handling the conversion, sometimes with rates up to 10% higher than usual.

KYOTO PACKING LIST

When packing for a trip to Kyoto, consider including the following items to ensure you're well-prepared for your adventure:

Clothing:
Light Layers: Kyoto experiences varying temperatures throughout the year, so pack lightweight, breathable clothing for the warmer months and layerable items for cooler weather.

Comfortable Shoes: Expect lots of walking on uneven surfaces, so bring sturdy and comfortable footwear, especially if planning to explore temples and gardens.

Rain Gear: Kyoto sees rain throughout the year, so a compact umbrella or a waterproof jacket can be incredibly handy.

Modest Attire: Some temples and shrines may require modest clothing, so pack attire that covers shoulders and knees.

Accessories:

Backpack or Day Bag: Ideal for carrying essentials during sightseeing.

Reusable Water Bottle: Stay hydrated while exploring.

Sun Protection: Sunscreen, sunglasses, and a wide-brimmed hat for protection against UV rays.

Portable Power Bank: Keep your devices charged for navigation and photography.

Travel Essentials:

Travel Adapter: Japan uses Type A and Type B electrical outlets.

Language Translator or Phrasebook: Helpful for basic communication.

Travel Insurance: Ensure coverage for any unforeseen circumstances, including health-related issues or trip cancellations.

Electronics:

Camera or Smartphone: Capture the beauty of Kyoto's landscapes and historic sites.

Chargers and Adapters: Keep all devices powered up.

Miscellaneous Items:

Cash and Cards: Have Japanese Yen on hand for smaller establishments that may not accept cards.

Medication and First Aid Kit: Include any necessary prescription medications and basic first aid supplies.

Reusable Shopping Bag: Useful for carrying souvenirs or groceries.

Towel and Toiletries: Travel-sized toiletries and a small towel for personal use.

Pocket Wi-Fi or SIM Card: Stay connected for navigation and communication.

Specific Seasonal Items:

Winter: Warm coat, gloves, scarf, and thermal clothing if visiting during the colder months.

Summer: Light, breathable clothing and insect repellent for the warmer, humid weather.

Remember to pack efficiently, keeping in mind the weather forecast and the activities you plan to undertake. Kyoto offers a rich tapestry of cultural experiences, and being well-prepared ensures you can fully immerse yourself in its wonders.

We have come to the end of this travel guide to Kyoto. Thanks for reading it up to the last page. I am hoping that it has fed you with helpful information to help you navigate Kyoto with ease. Rating this book and leaving an honest review will always be appreciated.

Printed in Great Britain
by Amazon

37114055R10096